GRADE 5

Phonics/Spelling
PRACTICE BOOK

Macmillan/McGraw-Hill

B

The McGraw·Hill Companies

Macmillan/McGraw-Hill

Published by Macmillan/McGraw-Hill, of McGraw-Hill Education, a division of The McGraw-Hill Companies, Inc., Two Penn Plaza, New York, New York 10121.

Printed in the United States of America

4 5 6 7 8 9 10 RHR 13 12 11

Contents

Unit 1 • Taking a Stand

Unit 2 • Investigations

Unit 3 • Using Your Wits

Unit 4 • Team Up to Survive

Unit 5 • The American West

Unit 6 • Changes

Name ____________________

Fold back the paper along the dotted line. Use the blanks to write each word as it is read aloud. When you finish the test, unfold the paper. Use the list at the right to correct any spelling mistakes.

1. ____________ 1. jut
2. ____________ 2. nick
3. ____________ 3. tenth
4. ____________ 4. shrug
5. ____________ 5. stuff
6. ____________ 6. sense
7. ____________ 7. damp
8. ____________ 8. cot
9. ____________ 9. fling
10. ____________ 10. notch
11. ____________ 11. gush
12. ____________ 12. scan
13. ____________ 13. batch
14. ____________ 14. rough
15. ____________ 15. stump
16. ____________ 16. tough
17. ____________ 17. laugh
18. ____________ 18. guess
19. ____________ 19. lead
20. ____________ 20. dove

Review Words

21. ____________ 21. past
22. ____________ 22. dock
23. ____________ 23. plum

Challenge Words

24. ____________ 24. cinch
25. ____________ 25. blond

Name ______________________________

Using the Word Study Steps

1. LOOK at the word.
2. SAY the word aloud.
3. STUDY the letters in the word.
4. WRITE the word.
5. CHECK the word.
   Did you spell the word right?
   If not, go back to step 1.

batch	dove	stuff	tenth	tough
nick	fling	notch	scan	stump
rough	shrug	jut	guess	laugh
lead	gush	damp	cot	sense

A. Find and Circle

Where are the spelling words?

d a m p e f g t e n t h w r t a r l t q g u e s s t u c o t z r
b r d s t u m p e l a u g h b z x e n i c k a r t s h r u g e t
s c a n t o u g h m t s a p b a t c h e y s e n s e g l u w a
g f l i n g i g u s h r o u g h h j u t a h c s t u f f d o v e
c k o d h w q l e a d v n o t c h c n i h c l o k m l p u e r

B. Alphabetical Order

Use the lines below to write the spelling words in alphabetical order.

1. ____________ 6. ____________ 11. ____________ 16. ____________
2. ____________ 7. ____________ 12. ____________ 17. ____________
3. ____________ 8. ____________ 13. ____________ 18. ____________
4. ____________ 9. ____________ 14. ____________ 19. ____________
5. ____________ 10. ____________ 15. ____________ 20. ____________

Name ____________________

batch	dove	stuff	tenth	tough
nick	fling	notch	scan	stump
rough	shrug	jut	guess	laugh
lead	gush	damp	cot	sense

Sort each spelling word by finding the sound and spelling pattern to which it belongs.

Short a spelled *a*

1. ____________
2. ____________
3. ____________

Short a spelled *au*

1. ____________

Short e spelled *e*

1. ____________
2. ____________

Short e spelled *ue*

1. ____________

Short e spelled *ea*

1. ____________

Short i spelled *i*

1. ____________
2. ____________

Short o spelled *o*

1. ____________
2. ____________

Short u spelled *u*

1. ____________
2. ____________
3. ____________
4. ____________
5. ____________

Short u spelled *o*

1. ____________

Short u spelled *ou*

1. ____________
2. ____________

Name ________________________________

batch	dove	stuff	tenth	tough
nick	fling	notch	scan	stump
rough	shrug	jut	guess	laugh
lead	gush	damp	cot	sense

Definitions

Write the spelling word that matches each definition below.

1. throw ________________
2. wet ________________
3. stick out ________________
4. pour out ________________
5. mark ________________
6. small bed ________________
7. bird ________________
8. small cut ________________
9. confuse ________________
10. not smooth ________________
11. group ________________
12. read quickly ________________

Finish the Sentences

Write the spelling word that best completes each sentence.

13. It was a ________________ word to spell.
14. The ________________ question was the hardest of all.
15. His answer did not make ________________.
16. She was happy and started to ________________.
17. She took a ________________ because she did not know the answer.
18. He was unsure and answered the question with a ________________.
19. He had too much ________________ in his desk.
20. She gave him a ________________ pencil for the test.

Name ______________________________

A. Circle the misspelled words in the set of instructions. Write the words correctly on the lines below.

You will receive a list of ten words for the spelling bee. Before the contest begins, skain the list of words. The tinth word on the list is a bonus word. Its spelling is unusual and may stumpe you. You will get an extra point if you spell the bonus word correctly.

Here are some tips for the contest. If a word does not make cents to you, ask to hear it again. If you are not sure how to spell a word, take a gess. Last but not least, don't worry if your hands feel dap. That just means you are feeling a little nervous.

1. ______________ 3. ______________ 5. ______________
2. ______________ 4. ______________ 6. ______________

B. Writing Activity

Have you ever watched or taken part in a contest? Write a description of what happened or what you think might happen at a contest, using four spelling words.

____
____
____
____
____
____
____
____
____
____
____

Name ____________________

Look at the words in each set below. One word in each set is spelled correctly. Use a pencil to fill in the circle next to the correct word. Before you begin, look at the sample set of words. Sample A has been done for you. Do Sample B by yourself. When you are sure you know what to do, you may go on with the rest of the page.

Sample A:
- Ⓐ lump
- Ⓑ lumpe
- Ⓒ lumpp
- Ⓓ luump

Sample B:
- Ⓔ tacke
- Ⓕ taak
- Ⓖ tack
- Ⓗ takk

1. Ⓐ batch Ⓑ bach Ⓒ baatch Ⓓ bache

2. Ⓔ rugh Ⓕ rughe Ⓖ rough Ⓗ rogh

3. Ⓐ stumpe Ⓑ stuump Ⓒ stummp Ⓓ stump

4. Ⓔ jutt Ⓕ jut Ⓖ chut Ⓗ juut

5. Ⓐ tough Ⓑ touff Ⓒ tuf Ⓓ tugh

6. Ⓔ nik Ⓕ nikke Ⓖ nicke Ⓗ nick

7. Ⓐ shrugg Ⓑ shrug Ⓒ shruge Ⓓ shruug

8. Ⓔ tenth Ⓕ teenth Ⓖ tenthe Ⓗ teenthe

9. Ⓐ stouff Ⓑ stuff Ⓒ stufe Ⓓ stuffe

10. Ⓔ lafe Ⓕ laagh Ⓖ lagh Ⓗ laugh

11. Ⓐ gess Ⓑ gues Ⓒ guess Ⓓ guss

12. Ⓔ sense Ⓕ senss Ⓖ sens Ⓗ seens

13. Ⓐ dampe Ⓑ dammp Ⓒ daamp Ⓓ damp

14. Ⓔ cott Ⓕ kott Ⓖ cot Ⓗ kot

15. Ⓐ fling Ⓑ flinge Ⓒ fliing Ⓓ faling

16. Ⓔ guush Ⓕ gushe Ⓖ gush Ⓗ gussh

17. Ⓐ dove Ⓑ duv Ⓒ duve Ⓓ dov

18. Ⓔ lead Ⓕ leede Ⓖ leade Ⓗ ledd

19. Ⓐ nootch Ⓑ noch Ⓒ notch Ⓓ noutch

20. Ⓔ scane Ⓕ scan Ⓖ scaan Ⓗ scahn

Name ____________________

Fold back the paper along the dotted line. Use the blanks to write each word as it is read aloud. When you finish the test, unfold the paper. Use the list at the right to correct any spelling mistakes.

	1. ________	1. paste
	2. ________	2. bride
	3. ________	3. shave
	4. ________	4. spice
	5. ________	5. greed
	6. ________	6. plead
	7. ________	7. greet
	8. ________	8. heap
	9. ________	9. paid
	10. ________	10. coach
	11. ________	11. theme
	12. ________	12. type
	13. ________	13. oak
	14. ________	14. growth
	15. ________	15. yolk
	16. ________	16. folks
	17. ________	17. aim
	18. ________	18. prey
	19. ________	19. tow
	20. ________	20. grind
Review Words	21. ________	21. tenth
	22. ________	22. damp
	23. ________	23. stuff
Challenge Words	24. ________	24. decay
	25. ________	25. lifetime

Name ____

Using the Word Study Steps

1. LOOK at the word.
2. SAY the word aloud.
3. STUDY the letters in the word.

Find Rhyming Words

Circle the word in each row that rhymes with the word in dark type.

1.	**bride**	raid	tide	rude
2.	**greet**	met	grunt	seat
3.	**shave**	wave	dove	shy
4.	**tow**	toe	too	saw
5.	**prey**	say	eye	pry
6.	**plead**	play	need	head
7.	**heap**	yap	heel	deep
8.	**oak**	joke	oat	neck
9.	**spice**	icy	nice	speck
10.	**type**	ripe	cup	twine
11.	**theme**	then	dream	some
12.	**paid**	pail	mad	parade
13.	**paste**	taste	pass	coast
14.	**aim**	lame	aid	may
15.	**greed**	great	weed	grand

Name ______________________________

folks	aim	prey	yolk	greed
greet	grind	growth	heap	coach
oak	paid	paste	plead	shave
theme	bride	tow	spice	type

Sort each spelling word by finding the sound and spelling pattern to which it belongs.

Write the words that have long *a* spelled:

ai	***a_e***	***ey***
1. ____________	**1.** ____________	**1.** ____________
2. ____________	**2.** ____________	

Write the words that have long *e* spelled:

ee	***ea***	***e_e***
1. ____________	**1.** ____________	**1.** ____________
2. ____________	**2.** ____________	

Write the words that have long *i* spelled:

i	***y***	***i_e***
1. ____________	**1.** ____________	**1.** ____________
		2. ____________

Write the words that have long *o* spelled:

o	***oa***	***ow***
1. ____________	**1.** ____________	**1.** ____________
2. ____________	**2.** ____________	**2.** ____________

Name ______________________________

folks	aim	prey	yolk	greed
greet	grind	growth	heap	coach
oak	paid	paste	plead	shave
theme	bride	tow	spice	type

Replacements

Write the spelling word that can replace the underlined word or words in each sentence below.

1. Adam wasn't like any kind of person she had ever met. ____________
2. He pulled up the weeds and threw them in a pile. ____________
3. Phil's new wife was as strong as he was. ____________
4. He used to say hello to people with a wave of his hand. ____________
5. His goal was to finish the race in record time. ____________
6. Pat did not want to be given money for anything he did. ____________
7. The message of the story is that good triumphs over evil. ____________
8. People everywhere had heard about the news. ____________

Definitions

Write the spelling word that matches each definition below.

9. part of an egg ____________
10. glue ____________
11. pull ____________
12. beg ____________
13. kind of tree ____________
14. crush ____________
15. hunted animal ____________
16. desire for a lot of something ____________
17. an increase in size ____________
18. cut off hair ____________
19. wagon pulled by horses ____________
20. something added to food ____________

Name ______________________________

A. Circle the misspelled words in the passage. Write the words correctly on the lines below.

Kendra and Sam decided to add a little twist to this year's fundraising event. Instead of making the same old food, they thought of a new theem: "Breakfast in Bed." Their ame is to raise enough money for the class trip to the city.

Their classmates grete people as they come to the cafeteria on Saturday morning. Many are still wearing their pajamas. Sam cooks each egg until the yoke is just right. Kendra asks diners if she can grined fresh pepper on top. Most fokes seem pretty happy with the meal. All in all, it looks like the event will be a huge success!

1. ____________ 3. ____________ 5. ____________
2. ____________ 4. ____________ 6. ____________

B. Writing Activity

Suppose that you were asked to raise money for an event. How would you do it? Write a short article about your plans. Use at least four spelling words.

Name ____

Look at the words in each set below. One word in each set is spelled correctly. Use a pencil to fill in the circle next to the correct word. Before you begin, look at the sample set of words. Sample A has been done for you. Do Sample B by yourself. When you are sure you know what to do, you may go on with the rest of the page.

Sample A:

Ⓐ doom
Ⓑ dume
Ⓒ duum
Ⓓ doome

Sample B:

Ⓔ taik
Ⓕ taak
Ⓖ take
Ⓗ tehk

1. Ⓐ fokes Ⓑ folks Ⓒ fokse Ⓓ fohks

2. Ⓔ ame Ⓕ aame Ⓖ aime Ⓗ aim

3. Ⓐ prey Ⓑ preye Ⓒ praiy Ⓓ prai

4. Ⓔ yok Ⓕ yolke Ⓖ yolk Ⓗ yohk

5. Ⓐ greed Ⓑ grede Ⓒ greid Ⓓ gried

6. Ⓔ grete Ⓕ greet Ⓖ greit Ⓗ griet

7. Ⓐ grinde Ⓑ grind Ⓒ gihnd Ⓓ griind

8. Ⓔ growth Ⓕ groath Ⓖ groeth Ⓗ grothe

9. Ⓐ heep Ⓑ hepe Ⓒ heap Ⓓ heape

10. Ⓔ coche Ⓕ coach Ⓖ coch Ⓗ coache

11. Ⓐ ohk Ⓑ oke Ⓒ oak Ⓓ ock

12. Ⓔ paid Ⓕ pade Ⓖ payed Ⓗ paad

13. Ⓐ paste Ⓑ paist Ⓒ paast Ⓓ paiste

14. Ⓔ pleed Ⓕ plede Ⓖ pleid Ⓗ plead

15. Ⓐ shaiv Ⓑ shave Ⓒ shav Ⓓ shaive

16. Ⓔ heem Ⓕ theim Ⓖ theeme Ⓗ theme

17. Ⓐ brid Ⓑ bride Ⓒ briid Ⓓ briide

18. Ⓔ toh Ⓕ towe Ⓖ tow Ⓗ tohe

19. Ⓐ spyce Ⓑ spihc Ⓒ spihce Ⓓ spice

20. Ⓔ tipe Ⓕ type Ⓖ tighp Ⓗ typ

Name ______________________

Fold back the paper along the dotted line. Use the blanks to write each word as it is read aloud. When you finish the test, unfold the paper. Use the list at the right to correct any spelling mistakes.

	1. ______	1. tuna
	2. ______	2. duty
	3. ______	3. lose
	4. ______	4. few
	5. ______	5. doom
	6. ______	6. bamboo
	7. ______	7. soothe
	8. ______	8. crooks
	9. ______	9. hoof
	10. ______	10. hooks
	11. ______	11. booth
	12. ______	12. handbook
	13. ______	13. prove
	14. ______	14. mute
	15. ______	15. amuse
	16. ______	16. plume
	17. ______	17. hue
	18. ______	18. view
	19. ______	19. bruise
	20. ______	20. union
Review Words	21. ______	21. theme
	22. ______	22. coach
	23. ______	23. bride
Challenge Words	24. ______	24. strewn
	25. ______	25. accuse

Name ______________________________

Using the Word Study Steps

1. LOOK at the word.
2. SAY the word aloud.
3. STUDY the letters in the word.

Find Rhyming Words

Circle the word in each row that rhymes with the word in dark type.

1. **lose**	choose	close	lost
2. **booth**	both	tooth	comb
3. **hue**	who	would	cue
4. **mute**	cute	mood	flunk
5. **duty**	sooty	fruity	dust
6. **view**	grow	shoes	few
7. **plume**	gloom	plunk	put
8. **soothe**	tow	smooth	root
9. **hooks**	moods	broke	brooks
10. **bruise**	brush	burn	cruise
11. **prove**	shove	move	dove
12. **doom**	room	dorm	dome
13. **hoof**	roof	half	woof
14. **few**	feud	stew	fool
15. **amuse**	confuse	amidst	among

Name ______________________________

amuse	bamboo	soothe	crooks	tuna
doom	few	view	hoof	hooks
hue	bruise	booth	lose	duty
handbook	prove	mute	plume	union

Sort each spelling word by finding the sound and spelling pattern to which it belongs.

Write the words that have /ü/ spelled:

u

1. ______________
2. ______________

o_e

1. ______________
2. ______________

u_e

1. ______________

oo

1. ______________
2. ______________
3. ______________
4. ______________

ui

1. ______________

Write the words that have /ū/ spelled:

u_e

1. ______________
2. ______________
3. ______________

u

1. ______________

ew

1. ______________
2. ______________

Write the words that have /u̇/ spelled:

oo

1. ______________
2. ______________
3. ______________
4. ______________

Name ______________________________

amuse	bamboo	soothe	crooks	tuna
doom	few	view	hoof	hooks
hue	bruise	booth	lose	duty
handbook	prove	mute	plume	union

Write the spelling word that best completes each sentence. Circle the *u* sound in each word. Use the word box to check your spelling.

1. Banana trees, rubber trees, and ______________ grow in tropical rain forests.
2. The new building will block our ______________ of the park.
3. A ______________ of smoke rose from the chimney.
4. ______________ people know how to fix computers.
5. Our team will ______________ if we don't practice hard.
6. It is everyone's ______________ to follow the rules.
7. The leaves have a beautiful ______________ in autumn.
8. He found the directions in a ______________ for new students.

Similar Meanings

Write the spelling word that has the same, or almost the same, meaning.

9. silent ______________
10. bump ______________
11. comfort ______________
12. animal foot ______________
13. entertain ______________
14. bent pieces of metal ______________
15. box-like space ______________
16. coming together ______________
17. show ______________
18. large fish ______________
19. disaster ______________
20. dishonest people ______________

Name ______________________________

A. Circle the misspelled words in the paragraph. Write the words correctly on the lines below.

Our backyard has only a fue trees. The big maple tree is my favorite. I have a good vyoo of it from my room. All the trees in the yard loos their leaves in the fall. Before that happens, though, their leaves change color. The maple's leaves turn a red hiew. I amewz myself by collecting maple leaves each fall. Once I found a ploom from a bird on the ground by the maple. I saved it along with the leaves I had collected.

1. ____________ 3. ____________ 5. ____________

2. ____________ 4. ____________ 6. ____________

B. Writing Activity

Write about something in nature that interests you. Use four spelling words in your description.

Name ______________________________

Look at the words in each set below. One word in each set is spelled correctly. Use a pencil to fill in the circle next to the correct word. Before you begin, look at the sample set of words. Sample A has been done for you. Do Sample B by yourself. When you are sure you know what to do, you may go on with the rest of the page.

Sample A:
- Ⓐ loot
- Ⓑ lut
- Ⓒ loote
- Ⓓ lote

Sample B:
- Ⓔ tock
- Ⓕ tuk
- Ⓖ took
- Ⓗ tuke

1. Ⓐ amuse Ⓑ amyuse Ⓒ amyoos Ⓓ amoose

2. Ⓔ bambu Ⓕ bamboo Ⓖ bambuu Ⓗ bambo

3. Ⓐ soothie Ⓑ soothe Ⓒ southe Ⓓ soohte

4. Ⓔ croks Ⓕ crokes Ⓖ crooks Ⓗ crookes

5. Ⓐ toona Ⓑ tuna Ⓒ tuuna Ⓓ tona

6. Ⓔ dume Ⓕ doom Ⓖ dum Ⓗ doome

7. Ⓐ fyoo Ⓑ few Ⓒ foo Ⓓ fu

8. Ⓔ vu Ⓕ vyoo Ⓖ view Ⓗ voo

9. Ⓐ huf Ⓑ hof Ⓒ hoof Ⓓ huuf

10. Ⓔ hucks Ⓕ hookes Ⓖ hukes Ⓗ hooks

11. Ⓐ hue Ⓑ hoo Ⓒ hyoo Ⓓ hu

12. Ⓔ bruise Ⓕ broose Ⓖ broos Ⓗ bruse

13. Ⓐ buthe Ⓑ boothe Ⓒ booth Ⓓ buth

14. Ⓔ lose Ⓕ loos Ⓖ luse Ⓗ lus

15. Ⓐ dootee Ⓑ duty Ⓒ dooty Ⓓ dutey

16. Ⓔ handbook Ⓕ handbuk Ⓖ handbooke Ⓗ handbuke

17. Ⓐ proove Ⓑ proov Ⓒ prove Ⓓ pruve

18. Ⓔ myoot Ⓕ moote Ⓖ mute Ⓗ miut

19. Ⓐ ploom Ⓑ plume Ⓒ ploome Ⓓ pluhm

20. Ⓔ oonon Ⓕ unon Ⓖ unun Ⓗ union

Name ____________________

Fold back the paper along the dotted line. Use the blanks to write each word as it is read aloud. When you finish the test, unfold the paper. Use the list at the right to correct any spelling mistakes.

	1. ________	1. heart
	2. ________	2. swear
	3. ________	3. aboard
	4. ________	4. squares
	5. ________	5. swore
	6. ________	6. chart
	7. ________	7. scorn
	8. ________	8. starch
	9. ________	9. source
	10. ________	10. fare
	11. ________	11. barge
	12. ________	12. thorn
	13. ________	13. marsh
	14. ________	14. force
	15. ________	15. harsh
	16. ________	16. scarce
	17. ________	17. coarse
	18. ________	18. flare
	19. ________	19. course
	20. ________	20. sword
Review Words	21. ________	21. soothe
	22. ________	22. prove
	23. ________	23. hoof
Challenge Words	24. ________	24. uproar
	25. ________	25. gorge

Name ______________________________

Using the Word Study Steps

1. LOOK at the word.
2. SAY the word aloud.
3. STUDY the letters in the word.
4. WRITE the word.
5. CHECK the word.
   Did you spell the word right?
   If not, go back to step 1.

force	scorn	sword	swore	source
aboard	course	coarse	chart	barge
harsh	marsh	starch	heart	scarce
squares	swear	flare	fare	thorn

Fill-Ins

A. Fill in the missing letters of each word to form a spelling word.

1. m ____ ____ sh
2. h ____ ____ ____ t
3. f ____ ____ e
4. st ____ ____ ch
5. th ____ ____ n
6. ab ____ ____ ____ d
7. squ ____ ____ es
8. sw ____ ____ e
9. f ____ ____ ce
10. sw ____ ____ r
11. c ____ ____ ____ se
12. sw ____ ____ d
13. b ____ ____ ge
14. h ____ ____ sh
15. sc ____ ____ n
16. sc ____ ____ ce
17. fl ____ ____ e
18. s ____ ____ ____ ce
19. c ____ ____ ____ se
20. ch ____ ____ t

Name ______________________________

force	scorn	sword	swore	source
aboard	course	coarse	chart	barge
harsh	marsh	starch	heart	scarce
squares	swear	flare	fare	thorn

Sort each spelling word by finding the sound and spelling pattern to which it belongs.

Write the words that have /är/ spelled:

ar

1. ______________

2. ______________

3. ______________

4. ______________

5. ______________

ear

1. ______________

Write the words that have /âr/ spelled:

are

1. ______________

2. ______________

3. ______________

ar

1. ______________

ear

1. ______________

Write the words that have /ôr/ spelled:

our

1. ______________

2. ______________

or

1. ______________

2. ______________

3. ______________

4. ______________

ore

1. ______________

oar

1. ______________

2. ______________

Name ____

Practice

Spelling: Words with *r*-controlled Vowels /är/, /âr/, /ôr/

force	scorn	sword	swore	source
aboard	course	coarse	chart	barge
harsh	marsh	starch	heart	scarce
squares	swear	flare	fare	thorn

Fill in the Blanks

Write the spelling word that best completes each sentence.

1. Only the sailors were allowed ______________ the boat.
2. Her ______________ beat quickly during the scary movie.
3. The horses ran around the ______________ twice.
4. The ______________ of the wind blew leaves out of the trees.
5. Our chores for each day are listed on a ______________.
6. The sun's rays ______________ across the water at dawn.
7. Her comments were ______________, so she apologized.
8. He ______________ that he would return to the seaside one day.

Related Words

Write the spelling word that is related to the sets of words below.

9. circles, triangles, ______________
10. rough, stiff, ______________
11. swamp, bog, ______________
12. needle, spike, ______________
13. soap, water, ______________
14. promise, pledge, ______________
15. blade, weapon, ______________
16. boat, ship, ______________
17. price, charge, ______________
18. rare, limited, ______________
19. hatred, dislike, ______________
20. beginning, cause, ______________

Name ______________________________

A. Circle the misspelled words in the message. Write the words correctly on the lines below.

Dear Tyra,

We have been abored the boat for two days now. Everything is going smoothly. We are right on corce to reach the next town. You can see where we are if you look at the cheart I gave you.

It's hard to describe what it felt like during the storm yesterday. The fours of the waves was incredible. Now it's calm, and we can see the flare of the bonfires along the beach. I sware my hart skipped a beat when we heard that the celebration had just begun. I'm so glad we made it in time!

I'll be home sooner than you think. Take care of your little brother!

Love, Dad

1. ______________ 3. ______________ 5. ______________

2. ______________ 4. ______________ 6. ______________

B. Writing Activity

Imagine that you are away from home. Write an e-mail message home to a friend or your family. Use four spelling words in your message.

____

____

____

____

____

____

____

____

____

Name ______________________________

Look at the words in each set below. One word in each set is spelled correctly. Use a pencil to fill in the circle next to the correct word. Before you begin, look at the sample set of words. Sample A has been done for you. Do Sample B by yourself. When you are sure you know what to do, you may go on with the rest of the page.

Sample A:

Ⓐ sort
Ⓑ soort
Ⓒ soorte
Ⓓ sorrt

Sample B:

Ⓔ sheare
Ⓕ shaar
Ⓖ share
Ⓗ shaare

1. Ⓐ force Ⓑ fohrce Ⓒ fors Ⓓ fource

2. Ⓔ skohrn Ⓕ scorne Ⓖ scorn Ⓗ skorn

3. Ⓐ sorde Ⓑ sword Ⓒ sord Ⓓ soord

4. Ⓔ swor Ⓕ sooor Ⓖ suore Ⓗ swore

5. Ⓐ sorce Ⓑ source Ⓒ sors Ⓓ sohrce

6. Ⓔ aboard Ⓕ abourd Ⓖ aborde Ⓗ abord

7. Ⓐ corse Ⓑ cohrs Ⓒ coarse Ⓓ coors

8. Ⓔ corse Ⓕ cohrs Ⓖ course Ⓗ coors

9. Ⓐ chort Ⓑ charte Ⓒ chart Ⓓ chorte

10. Ⓔ borje Ⓕ barg Ⓖ barge Ⓗ bahrge

11. Ⓐ horsh Ⓑ harshe Ⓒ haarsh Ⓓ harsh

12. Ⓔ marsh Ⓕ maarsh Ⓖ morsh Ⓗ marshe

13. Ⓐ staarch Ⓑ starche Ⓒ starch Ⓓ storch

14. Ⓔ haart Ⓕ hahrt Ⓖ heart Ⓗ harte

15. Ⓐ scarce Ⓑ scaerce Ⓒ scearce Ⓓ scarc

16. Ⓔ skwaers Ⓕ squares Ⓖ squeres Ⓗ squarez

17. Ⓐ sware Ⓑ swar Ⓒ swear Ⓓ swere

18. Ⓔ flaere Ⓕ flar Ⓖ flare Ⓗ flaer

19. Ⓐ faer Ⓑ faar Ⓒ fare Ⓓ fer

20. Ⓔ thorne Ⓕ thorn Ⓖ thohrn Ⓗ thourn

Name ______________________

Fold back the paper along the dotted line. Use the blanks to write each word as it is read aloud. When you finish the test, unfold the paper. Use the list at the right to correct any spelling mistakes.

	1. ______	1. clear
	2. ______	2. nerve
	3. ______	3. squirt
	4. ______	4. verse
	5. ______	5. surf
	6. ______	6. lurk
	7. ______	7. year
	8. ______	8. stern
	9. ______	9. spurts
	10. ______	10. lurch
	11. ______	11. blurt
	12. ______	12. thirst
	13. ______	13. spur
	14. ______	14. engineer
	15. ______	15. jeer
	16. ______	16. sneer
	17. ______	17. dreary
	18. ______	18. squirm
	19. ______	19. swerve
	20. ______	20. yearns
Review Words	21. ______	21. aboard
	22. ______	22. barge
	23. ______	23. scarce
Challenge Words	24. ______	24. smear
	25. ______	25. rehearse

Name ______________________________________

Practice

Spelling: *r*-Controlled Vowels *ur, er, ir, ear, eer*

Using the Word Study Steps

1. LOOK at the word.
2. SAY the word aloud.
3. STUDY the letters in the word.
4. WRITE the word.
5. CHECK the word.
   Did you spell the word right?
   If not, go back to step 1.

squirm	dreary	nerve	squirt	verse
surf	lurk	swerve	stern	spurts
lurch	blurt	thirst	spur	engineer
jeer	sneer	clear	year	yearns

A. Where Are the Spelling Words?

Find and circle the spelling words in this puzzle. Write each word below the puzzle.

a m s p u r t s o k y e a r j e e r y u q e b l u r t j a
l u r k g r i e n g i n e e r o a n e r v e s q u i r t o s
a e r d r e a r y c e t h i r s t o g s p u r e v s u r f f r
s n e e r a s w e r v e u n v e r s e i b n e r s t e r n w
o r l u r c h y e a r n s i m a c l e a r p a s q u i r m a

1. __________ 6. __________ 11. __________ 16. __________
2. __________ 7. __________ 12. __________ 17. __________
3. __________ 8. __________ 13. __________ 18. __________
4. __________ 9. __________ 14. __________ 19. __________
5. __________ 10. __________ 15. __________ 20. __________

Name ______________________________

squirm	dreary	nerve	squirt	verse
surf	lurk	swerve	stern	spurts
lurch	blurt	thirst	spur	engineer
jeer	sneer	clear	year	yearns

Sort each spelling word by finding the sound and spelling pattern to which it belongs.

Write the words that have /ûr/ spelled:

er

1. ______________
2. ______________
3. ______________
4. ______________

ir

1. ______________
2. ______________
3. ______________

ur

1. ______________
2. ______________
3. ______________
4. ______________
5. ______________
6. ______________

ear

1. ______________

Write the words that have /îr/ spelled:

ear

1. ______________
2. ______________
3. ______________

eer

1. ______________
2. ______________
3. ______________

Name ____________________

squirm	dreary	nerve	squirt	verse
surf	lurk	swerve	stern	spurts
lurch	blurt	thirst	spur	engineer
jeer	sneer	clear	year	yearns

Opposites

Write the spelling word whose meaning is the opposite of each clue below.

1. smiling ____________

2. applaud ____________

3. cheery ____________

4. be still ____________

5. cloudy ____________

6. smile warmly ____________

Fill in the Blank

Write the spelling word that best completes each sentence.

7. Every hungry person ____________ to be fed.

8. Gretchen did not have the ____________ to approach the bully.

9. He would often ____________ in the shadows of the buildings.

10. We didn't win the trophy, but we'll try again next ____________.

11. The dogs would ____________ at anyone who passed by.

12. The water came out in ____________ from the clogged hose.

13. Angela would ____________ out whatever she was thinking.

14. Tim had to ____________ to avoid hitting the boulder.

15. Tina tried to ____________ the horse into a gallop.

16. It would take an ____________ to fix the old bridge.

17. We went to the beach for some fun in the ____________.

18. She liked to ____________ frosting onto the cakes.

19. Playing in the sun gave us a great ____________ for water.

20. Jennifer sang a ____________ of her favorite song to him.

A. Circle the misspelled words in the diary entry below. Write the words correctly on the lines below.

Dear Diary,

Yesterday was a cold and drerey day, but at least it snowed last night. Today we had our first chance to go sledding all yeer. It took me a while to get up the nirve to start from the top of the hill. Once I made sure that the path was cleer, I started off. What a thrill to lerch forward at such a great speed! I could use more practice steering, though. At the bottom of the hill, I had to swurve hard to avoid hitting a tree!

1. ____________ 3. ____________ 5. ____________

2. ____________ 4. ____________ 6. ____________

B. Writing Activity

Write a paragraph about an activity that you would enjoy in either summer or winter. Use four words from the spelling list.

____

____

____

____

____

____

____

____

____

____

____

Name ______________________________

Look at the words in each set below. One word in each set is spelled correctly. Use a pencil to fill in the circle next to the correct word. Before you begin, look at the sample set of words. Sample A has been done for you. Do Sample B by yourself. When you are sure you know what to do, you may go on with the rest of the page.

Sample A:

Ⓐ first
Ⓑ furst
Ⓒ foorst
Ⓓ fuhrst

Sample B:

Ⓔ deir
Ⓕ dere
Ⓖ deer
Ⓗ der

1. Ⓐ skwirm Ⓑ squirm Ⓒ sqirm Ⓓ sqoorm

2. Ⓔ dreery Ⓕ drery Ⓖ dreary Ⓗ drerey

3. Ⓐ nerve Ⓑ nurv Ⓒ nirv Ⓓ nirve

4. Ⓔ skwirt Ⓕ sqirt Ⓖ sqoort Ⓗ squirt

5. Ⓐ verss Ⓑ virse Ⓒ verse Ⓓ virs

6. Ⓔ surf Ⓕ sirf Ⓖ soorf Ⓗ surfe

7. Ⓐ lurk Ⓑ loork Ⓒ lurke Ⓓ lerke

8. Ⓔ swurve Ⓕ swurv Ⓖ swerve Ⓗ swirve

9. Ⓐ stirn Ⓑ sturne Ⓒ sturn Ⓓ stern

10. Ⓔ spurtes Ⓕ sperts Ⓖ spurts Ⓗ spourts

11. Ⓐ lirtch Ⓑ lirch Ⓒ lurche Ⓓ lurch

12. Ⓔ blurt Ⓕ blirt Ⓖ blerte Ⓗ blert

13. Ⓐ thurst Ⓑ therst Ⓒ thirst Ⓓ thirste

14. Ⓔ spir Ⓕ spurre Ⓖ spur Ⓗ spuhr

15. Ⓐ engineer Ⓑ enginire Ⓒ enginir Ⓓ enginere

16. Ⓔ jeir Ⓕ jere Ⓖ jeer Ⓗ jir

17. Ⓐ snir Ⓑ sneer Ⓒ snere Ⓓ snear

18. Ⓔ clir Ⓕ cleer Ⓖ clere Ⓗ clear

19. Ⓐ yir Ⓑ yeer Ⓒ yere Ⓓ year

20. Ⓔ yurns Ⓕ yearns Ⓖ yirns Ⓗ yerns

Name ______________________

Fold back the paper along the dotted line. Use the blanks to write each word as it is read aloud. When you finish the test, unfold the paper. Use the list at the right to correct any spelling mistakes.

1. ______ 1. joint
2. ______ 2. foul
3. ______ 3. coil
4. ______ 4. hoist
5. ______ 5. stout
6. ______ 6. dawdle
7. ______ 7. mouthful
8. ______ 8. counter
9. ______ 9. brought
10. ______ 10. bawl
11. ______ 11. fountain
12. ______ 12. sprawls
13. ______ 13. douse
14. ______ 14. clause
15. ______ 15. sprouts
16. ______ 16. cautious
17. ______ 17. turmoil
18. ______ 18. scrawny
19. ______ 19. foundation
20. ______ 20. turquoise

Review Words

21. ______ 21. year
22. ______ 22. thirst
23. ______ 23. squirm

Challenge Words

24. ______ 24. buoyant
25. ______ 25. renown

Name ___________________________________

Practice

Spelling: Words with /ô/, /oi/, /ou/

Using the Word Study Steps

1. LOOK at the word.
2. SAY the word aloud.
3. STUDY the letters in the word.
4. WRITE the word.
5. CHECK the word. Did you spell the word right? If not, go back to step 1.

bawl	brought	cautious	counter
coil	foul	foundation	fountain
joint	mouthful	dawdle	sprawls
sprouts	turmoil	stout	hoist
clause	turquoise	douse	scrawny

Here and There

Circle the spelling words in this puzzle. Each word appears once.

B	J	F	O	U	N	D	A	T	I	O	N	F
R	M	O	U	T	H	F	U	L	N	M	R	O
O	L	U	T	U	R	Q	U	O	I	S	E	U
U	K	L	X	B	A	W	L	P	R	T	Q	N
G	J	C	A	U	T	I	O	U	S	O	B	T
H	O	I	S	T	W	E	R	T	B	U	H	A
T	I	C	P	U	H	X	D	H	A	T	Y	I
D	N	L	R	R	S	P	R	A	W	L	S	N
O	T	A	O	M	B	C	O	I	L	V	Z	G
U	A	U	U	O	C	O	U	N	T	E	R	H
S	B	S	T	I	N	S	C	R	A	W	N	Y
E	R	E	S	L	V	D	A	W	D	L	E	C

Name ____________________

bawl	brought	cautious	counter
coil	foul	foundation	fountain
joint	mouthful	dawdle	sprawls
sprouts	turmoil	stout	hoist
clause	turquoise	douse	scrawny

Sort each spelling word by finding the sound and spelling pattern to which it belongs.

Write the words with the sound /ô/ spelled:

aw

1. ____________
2. ____________
3. ____________
4. ____________

au

5. ____________
6. ____________

ou

7. ____________

Write the words with the /ou/ sound:

8. ____________
9. ____________
10. ____________
11. ____________
12. ____________
13. ____________
14. ____________
15. ____________

Write the words with the /oi/ sound:

16. ____________
17. ____________
18. ____________
19. ____________
20. ____________

Name ____________________

bawl	brought	cautious	counter
coil	foul	foundation	fountain
joint	mouthful	dawdle	sprawls
sprouts	turmoil	stout	hoist
clause	turquoise	douse	scrawny

A. Analogies

An analogy shows how two word pairs are similar. For example, *up* is to *down* as *in* is to *out*. Use spelling words to complete the analogies below. Use the word box to check your spelling.

1. **desk** is to **office** as ____________ is to **store**
2. **hot** is to **cold** as **hurry** is to ____________
3. **corner** is to **wall** as ____________ is to **arm**
4. **shingle** is to **roof** as **brick** is to ____________
5. **car** is to **metal** as **ring** is to ____________
6. **sprinkle** is to **rain** as ____________ is to **plants**
7. **took** is to **take** as ____________ is to **bring**
8. **book** is to **paper** as ____________ is to **water**
9. **house** is to **home** as **stretches** is to ____________
10. **drawer** is to **dresser** as ____________ is to **writing**

B. Antonyms

Write the spelling word that is the *opposite* of each word below.

11. dry ____________
12. release ____________
13. careless ____________
14. small taste ____________
15. slender ____________
16. peace ____________
17. enormous ____________
18. laugh ____________
19. drop ____________
20. fair ____________

Name ______________________________

A. Circle the misspelled words in this paragraph. Write the words correctly on the lines below.

Lupe loved to work in her island garden. She checked it every morning, looking for sprowts of vegetables and flowers. First she would douwse the plants with water. Then she sampled a mouthful of fresh tomatoes. She broght fresh flowers in and put them on the kitchen counter. Her grandmother taught her to take long-stemmed flowers and coyle them into a crown. Sometimes it was fun to daudle in the garden, and enjoy the sound of water in the fauntain.

1. ______________ 3. ______________ 5. ______________

2. ______________ 4. ______________ 6. ______________

B. Writing Activity

Can you imagine a beautiful park? Write a description of the park and what you might do there. Use four spelling words in your description.

____

____

____

____

____

____

____

____

____

____

____

____

____

Name ____________________

Look at the words in each set below. One word in each set is spelled correctly. Use a pencil to fill in the circle next to the correct word. Before you begin, look at the sample set of words. Sample A has been done for you. Do Sample B by yourself. When you are sure you know what to do, you may go on with the rest of the page.

Sample A:

Ⓐ baut
Ⓑ bouht
Ⓒ bought
Ⓓ bawt

Sample B:

Ⓔ spoil
Ⓕ spoyl
Ⓖ spoile
Ⓗ spoyel

1. Ⓐ baull Ⓑ baul Ⓒ bawll Ⓓ bawl

2. Ⓔ braut Ⓕ brought Ⓖ brouht Ⓗ braught

3. Ⓐ cautious Ⓑ caushious Ⓒ cautieous Ⓓ cawtious

4. Ⓔ cownter Ⓕ caunter Ⓖ counter Ⓗ cowntir

5. Ⓐ coil Ⓑ coyl Ⓒ coyel Ⓓ coile

6. Ⓔ faul Ⓕ foul Ⓖ foull Ⓗ faull

7. Ⓐ foundashen Ⓑ fowndation Ⓒ foundation Ⓓ foundatien

8. Ⓔ fowntain Ⓕ fountain Ⓖ founten Ⓗ fownten

9. Ⓐ joint Ⓑ joynt Ⓒ gioint Ⓓ goint

10. Ⓔ mouthfull Ⓕ mauthful Ⓖ mouthful Ⓗ mowthful

11. Ⓐ dawdle Ⓑ dawdel Ⓒ daudle Ⓓ daudlle

12. Ⓔ sprauls Ⓕ sprawlz Ⓖ sprawls Ⓗ sprols

13. Ⓐ sprowtts Ⓑ sproutts Ⓒ sprowts Ⓓ sprouts

14. Ⓔ turmoil Ⓕ termoil Ⓖ tirmoil Ⓗ turmmoil

15. Ⓐ staut Ⓑ stoute Ⓒ stout Ⓓ stoutt

16. Ⓔ hoyst Ⓕ hoiset Ⓖ hoiste Ⓗ hoist

17. Ⓐ clause Ⓑ claus Ⓒ clauze Ⓓ clauz

18. Ⓔ terquoise Ⓕ turquoise Ⓖ turquoyse Ⓗ turquoize

19. Ⓐ dous Ⓑ douce Ⓒ dawse Ⓓ douse

20. Ⓔ skronny Ⓕ skrawny Ⓖ scrawny Ⓗ schrawny

Name ____________________

Fold back the paper along the dotted line. Use the blanks to write each word as it is read aloud. When you finish the test, unfold the paper. Use the list at the right to correct any spelling mistakes.

1. ________ 1. rattlers
2. ________ 2. fangs
3. ________ 3. countries
4. ________ 4. liberties
5. ________ 5. potatoes
6. ________ 6. rodeos
7. ________ 7. taxes
8. ________ 8. reptiles
9. ________ 9. surroundings
10. ________ 10. beliefs
11. ________ 11. difficulties
12. ________ 12. batches
13. ________ 13. abilities
14. ________ 14. lashes
15. ________ 15. identities
16. ________ 16. losses
17. ________ 17. possibilities
18. ________ 18. notches
19. ________ 19. zeroes
20. ________ 20. eddies

Review Words

21. ________ 21. brought
22. ________ 22. counter
23. ________ 23. coil

Challenge Words

24. ________ 24. mangoes
25. ________ 25. sinews

Name ______________________________

Using the Word Study Steps

1. LOOK at the word.
2. SAY the word aloud.
3. STUDY the letters in the word.
4. WRITE the word.
5. CHECK the word.
   Did you spell the word right?
   If not, go back to step 1.

X the Words

Put an X on the one word in each line that does not fit the spelling pattern.

1. liberties	possibilities	zeroes	abilities
2. fangs	countries	rodeos	beliefs
3. batches	rattlers	reptiles	fangs
4. lashes	potatoes	identities	notches
5. difficulties	eddies	possibilities	rodeos
6. taxes	abilities	losses	notches
7. reptiles	batches	taxes	potatoes
8. beliefs	rodeos	rattlers	difficulties
9. countries	identities	surroundings	eddies
10. losses	zeroes	lashes	liberties

Name ______________________________

abilities	countries	batches	difficulties	eddies
fangs	identities	lashes	liberties	notches
possibilities	rattlers	reptiles	rodeos	surroundings
taxes	losses	potatoes	zeroes	beliefs

Pattern Power!

Sort the spelling words by finding the spelling pattern to which each belongs.

-es

1. ______________
2. ______________
3. ______________
4. ______________
5. ______________
6. ______________
7. ______________

-ies

1. ______________
2. ______________
3. ______________
4. ______________
5. ______________
6. ______________
7. ______________

-s

1. ______________
2. ______________
3. ______________
4. ______________
5. ______________

no change

1. ______________

Name ______________________________

abilities	countries	batches	difficulties	eddies
fangs	identities	lashes	liberties	notches
possibilities	rattlers	reptiles	rodeos	surroundings
taxes	losses	potatoes	zeroes	beliefs

Fill in the Blanks

Write the spelling word that best completes each sentence. Use the word box to check your spelling.

1. The water whirled around in the ______________.
2. Rattlesnakes live in several ______________ with different climates.
3. Miranda enjoyed making mashed ______________ with gravy.
4. The spy had several different ______________ to fool his enemies.
5. Snakes can be found at the zoo with other ______________.
6. The number one million contains six ______________.
7. Rattlers are more aware of their ______________ than people are.
8. The team had ten wins and three ______________ in the season.

Similar Meanings

Write the spelling word that has the same, or almost the same, meaning.

9. talents ______________
10. freedoms ______________
11. snakes ______________
12. values ______________
13. money raised by government ______________
14. snakes' teeth ______________
15. cowboy entertainment ______________
16. problems ______________
17. eye protection ______________
18. groups ______________
19. suggestions ______________
20. cuts ______________

Name ________________________________

A. Circle each misspelled word in this report. Write the correctly spelled word on the lines below.

Americans are asked to help their government according to their abilitys. In the United States, as in many other countreys, this means that people must pay taxs. The government uses the money to help citizens, build projects, and defend our libertyes. Sometimes paying the government causes difficultyes, especially if businesses have had losss during the year.

1. ____________ 3. ____________ 5. ____________
2. ____________ 4. ____________ 6. ____________

B. Writing Activity

Write a short report about snakes. Use four spelling words in your writing.

____
____
____
____
____
____
____
____
____
____
____
____
____

Name ______________________________

Look at the words in each set below. One word in each set is spelled correctly. Use a pencil to fill in the circle next to the correct word. Before you begin, look at the sample set of words. Sample A has been done for you. Do Sample B by yourself. When you are sure you know what to do, you may go on with the rest of the page.

Sample A:

Ⓐ scraches
Ⓑ scratches
Ⓒ skratches
Ⓓ scratchis

Sample B:

Ⓔ snakes
Ⓕ snakies
Ⓖ snaks
Ⓗ snaiks

1. Ⓐ abilitys Ⓑ abilitees Ⓒ abilities Ⓓ abbilities

2. Ⓔ countries Ⓕ countrys Ⓖ contries Ⓗ countrees

3. Ⓐ batches Ⓑ batchs Ⓒ batchess Ⓓ baches

4. Ⓔ difficultys Ⓕ dificulties Ⓖ difficulties Ⓗ difficullties

5. Ⓐ eddys Ⓑ eddeys Ⓒ edies Ⓓ eddies

6. Ⓔ fangz Ⓕ fangs Ⓖ fanges Ⓗ fanegs

7. Ⓐ identitees Ⓑ identitys Ⓒ identities Ⓓ iddentities

8. Ⓔ lashes Ⓕ lashs Ⓖ lashus Ⓗ lasshes

9. Ⓐ libertees Ⓑ libberties Ⓒ libertys Ⓓ liberties

10. Ⓔ notchs Ⓕ notchas Ⓖ notches Ⓗ noches

11. Ⓐ possibilities Ⓑ possabilities Ⓒ posibilities Ⓓ possibleities

12. Ⓔ rattleres Ⓕ rattlers Ⓖ ratlers Ⓗ rattllers

13. Ⓐ reptyles Ⓑ reptils Ⓒ reptiles Ⓓ repptiles

14. Ⓔ rodeos Ⓕ rodeoes Ⓖ rodios Ⓗ rodeose

15. Ⓐ surroundings Ⓑ suroundings Ⓒ surrounddings Ⓓ surrounndings

16. Ⓔ taxs Ⓕ taxes Ⓖ tackses Ⓗ taxxes

17. Ⓐ lossses Ⓑ lossses Ⓒ losses Ⓓ lausses

18. Ⓔ pitatoes Ⓕ patatoes Ⓖ potaitoes Ⓗ potatoes

19. Ⓐ zerose Ⓑ zeroes Ⓒ zerros Ⓓ zerroes

20. Ⓔ beleafs Ⓕ beleefs Ⓖ beliefs Ⓗ biliefs

Fold back the paper along the dotted line. Use the blanks to write each word as it is read aloud. When you finish the test, unfold the paper. Use the list at the right to correct any spelling mistakes.

	1. ______	1. jogging
	2. ______	2. dripping
	3. ______	3. skimmed
	4. ______	4. accepted
	5. ______	5. amusing
	6. ______	6. easing
	7. ______	7. regretted
	8. ______	8. forbidding
	9. ______	9. referred
	10. ______	10. injured
	11. ______	11. deserved
	12. ______	12. applied
	13. ______	13. relied
	14. ______	14. renewing
	15. ______	15. complicated
	16. ______	16. qualified
	17. ______	17. threatening
	18. ______	18. gnarled
	19. ______	19. envied
	20. ______	20. fascinated
Review Words	21. ______	21. difficulties
	22. ______	22. notches
	23. ______	23. rodeos
Challenge Words	24. ______	24. adoring
	25. ______	25. diaries

Name ____

Using the Word Study Steps

1. LOOK at the word.
2. SAY the word aloud.
3. STUDY the letters in the word.
4. WRITE the word.
5. CHECK the word.
Did you spell the word right?
If not, go back to step 1.

qualified	renewing	skimmed	gnarled
threatening	envied	deserved	amusing
dripping	complicated	forbidding	relied
regretted	injured	applied	easing
accepted	referred	jogging	fascinated

A. Find and Circle

Find and circle each of the spelling words in this puzzle. Words may read forward, backward, upward, downward, or diagonally.

G	Q	A	D	S	L	F	M	R	G	D	A	R	Z	T	J	Y	C
N	U	P	E	K	F	F	A	N	E	K	B	M	G	Q	F	O	O
I	A	P	I	Y	B	S	I	T	D	E	V	R	E	S	E	D	M
N	L	L	V	X	I	W	A	D	E	T	T	E	R	G	E	R	P
E	I	I	N	V	E	N	G	N	I	K	A	R	B	G	K	D	L
T	F	E	E	N	I	D	R	I	P	P	I	N	G	N	G	E	I
A	I	D	E	C	G	N	I	S	U	M	A	S	E	A	N	M	C
E	E	R	S	O	I	N	J	U	R	E	D	N	A	R	I	M	A
R	D	A	D	E	I	L	E	R	C	O	K	G	S	L	G	I	T
H	F	F	O	R	B	I	D	D	I	N	G	S	I	E	G	K	E
T	P	R	G	D	D	E	R	R	E	F	E	R	N	D	O	S	D
A	C	C	E	P	T	E	D	R	X	Y	Q	N	G	S	J	Q	R

Name ______________________________

qualified	renewing	skimmed	gnarled
threatening	envied	deserved	amusing
dripping	complicated	forbidding	relied
regretted	injured	applied	easing
accepted	referred	jogging	fascinated

Sort each spelling word according to its ending. Write the spelling words that end in:

-ed

1. ____________________
2. ____________________
3. ____________________
4. ____________________
5. ____________________
6. ____________________
7. ____________________
8. ____________________
9. ____________________
10. ____________________
11. ____________________
12. ____________________
13. ____________________

Write the spelling words that end in:

-ing

1. ____________________
2. ____________________
3. ____________________
4. ____________________
5. ____________________
6. ____________________
7. ____________________

Name ______________________________

qualified	renewing	skimmed	gnarled
threatening	envied	deserved	amusing
dripping	complicated	forbidding	relied
regretted	injured	applied	easing
accepted	referred	jogging	fascinated

Definitions

Write the spelling word that has the same, or almost the same, meaning.

1. depended ________________
2. amazed ________________
3. funny ________________
4. hard to understand or handle ________________
5. hurt ________________
6. running lightly ________________
7. able; prepared for something ________________
8. twisted; full of knots ________________
9. read quickly ________________

Sentence Completions

Complete each sentence with a spelling word. Use the word box to check your spelling.

10. The inventors ________________ to have a monument built in their honor.
11. The family thought about ________________ their subscriptions.
12. The people who had to work ________________ those who had the day off.
13. The article ________________ to the volunteers who helped out.
14. The artist ________________ an award for her work.

A. Circle the misspelled words in the passage. Write the words correctly on the lines below.

Dr. Martin stood there, getting ready to give her speech. She skimd her notes, making sure that nothing was missing. She had applide for the grant three weeks ago, knowing that she was qualifide. Now that she worked at the research center, she regrettid not knowing about the grant sooner. She began her speech with an amyusing story to relieve some of the pressure. Within minutes, the audience was fassinated.

1. ______________ 3. ______________ 5. ______________

2. ______________ 4. ______________ 6. ______________

Writing Activity

B. Write a paragraph about a grant or award that you would like to receive for a possible project. Use four words from your spelling list.

____

____

____

____

____

____

____

____

____

____

____

____

____

Name ______________________________

Look at the words in each set below. One word in each set is spelled correctly. Use a pencil to fill in the circle next to the correct word. Before you begin, look at the sample set of words. Sample A has been done for you. Do Sample B by yourself. When you are sure you know what to do, you may go on with the rest of the page.

Sample A:

Ⓐ runnning
Ⓑ runing
Ⓒ running
Ⓓ rhunning

Sample B:

Ⓔ amazed
Ⓕ umazed
Ⓖ ammazed
Ⓗ amazzed

1. Ⓐ amusing Ⓑ ammusing Ⓒ amussing Ⓓ ammussing

2. Ⓔ applied Ⓕ apllyed Ⓖ aplied Ⓗ appllied

3. Ⓐ complicatted Ⓑ complikated Ⓒ commplicated Ⓓ complicated

4. Ⓔ daserved Ⓕ diserved Ⓖ deserved Ⓗ desserved

5. Ⓐ driping Ⓑ dripping Ⓒ drippping Ⓓ drihping

6. Ⓔ easing Ⓕ easeing Ⓖ eazing Ⓗ eazeing

7. Ⓐ envyed Ⓑ enveyed Ⓒ envied Ⓓ enveed

8. Ⓔ fascanated Ⓕ facinated Ⓖ fassinated Ⓗ fascinated

9. Ⓐ forbidding Ⓑ forbiding Ⓒ forebidding Ⓓ fourbidding

10. Ⓔ narled Ⓕ gnarld Ⓖ narld Ⓗ gnarled

11. Ⓐ injured Ⓑ enjured Ⓒ injurd Ⓓ ingerred

12. Ⓔ joggging Ⓕ joging Ⓖ jogging Ⓗ joggeng

13. Ⓐ quallified Ⓑ qualified Ⓒ qualafied Ⓓ qualefied

14. Ⓔ ascepted Ⓕ acsepted Ⓖ accepted Ⓗ ackseptd

15. Ⓐ regretted Ⓑ regreted Ⓒ reggretted Ⓓ rigretted

16. Ⓔ rilied Ⓕ rellied Ⓖ realied Ⓗ relied

17. Ⓐ rinewing Ⓑ rennewing Ⓒ renewing Ⓓ reneweing

18. Ⓔ skimmed Ⓕ skimed Ⓖ skimmd Ⓗ scimmed

19. Ⓐ thretening Ⓑ threatning Ⓒ threataning Ⓓ threatening

20. Ⓔ riferred Ⓕ refered Ⓖ referred Ⓗ refurred

Name ______________________________

Fold back the paper along the dotted line. Use the blanks to write each word as it is read aloud. When you finish the test, unfold the paper. Use the list at the right to correct any spelling mistakes.

	1. ____________	1. you've
	2. ____________	2. she'd
	3. ____________	3. that's
	4. ____________	4. what's
	5. ____________	5. doesn't
	6. ____________	6. there's
	7. ____________	7. you're
	8. ____________	8. wasn't
	9. ____________	9. we'll
	10. ____________	10. we've
	11. ____________	11. we're
	12. ____________	12. couldn't
	13. ____________	13. I've
	14. ____________	14. didn't
	15. ____________	15. they're
	16. ____________	16. shouldn't
	17. ____________	17. wouldn't
	18. ____________	18. he'd
	19. ____________	19. don't
	20. ____________	20. isn't
Review Words	21. ____________	21. dripping
	22. ____________	22. applied
	23. ____________	23. diaries
Challenge Words	24. ____________	24. won't
	25. ____________	25. aren't

Name ______________________________

Using the Word Study Steps

1. LOOK at the word.
2. SAY the word aloud.
3. STUDY the letters in the word.
4. WRITE the word.
5. CHECK the word. Did you spell the word right? If not, go back to step 1.

you've	doesn't	we'll	I've	wouldn't
she'd	there's	we've	didn't	he'd
that's	you're	we're	they're	don't
what's	wasn't	couldn't	shouldn't	isn't

A. Word Combining

Combine the two short words to write a spelling word.

1. you + have = ______________
2. would + not = ______________
3. do + not = ______________
4. we + will = ______________
5. they + are = ______________
6. could + not = ______________
7. we + are = ______________
8. I + have = ______________
9. there + is = ______________
10. does + not = ______________

B. Fill in the missing letters to write a spelling word. You will use one of the blanks for the apostrophe.

11. y ___ u ___ r ___
12. d ___ d n ___ t
13. h ___ ___ d
14. i ___ ___ ___ t
15. w ___ ___ t ___ s

Name ______________________________

you've	doesn't	we'll	I've	wouldn't
she'd	there's	we've	didn't	he'd
that's	you're	we're	they're	don't
what's	wasn't	couldn't	shouldn't	isn't

Sort the spelling words by contraction endings.

'd

1. ______________
2. ______________

's

1. ______________
2. ______________
3. ______________

've

1. ______________
2. ______________
3. ______________

'll

1. ______________

n't

1. ______________
2. ______________
3. ______________
4. ______________
5. ______________
6. ______________
7. ______________
8. ______________

're

1. ______________
2. ______________
3. ______________

Name ______________________________

you've	doesn't	we'll	I've	wouldn't
she'd	there's	we've	didn't	he'd
that's	you're	we're	they're	don't
what's	wasn't	couldn't	shouldn't	isn't

A. Fill in the Blank

Write the spelling word that best completes each sentence. Use the word box to check your spelling.

1. Calling people names ______________ a good way to make friends.
2. ______________ read some books about airplanes, haven't you?
3. Here's a story ______________ about other kinds of flying.
4. ______________ this a picture of?
5. ______________ looking at a picture of outer space, aren't you?
6. ______________ heard that new hit song, haven't we?
7. Jen and I like mysteries. ______________ reading about a theft.
8. ______________ a chance of rain today, isn't there?
9. ______________ wait for the bus at the corner.
10. ______________ read about game creators next.
11. "______________ heard he was cast in the play," I tell Jen.
12. Jen said that ______________ like to see the performance.
13. I like amusement parks. ______________ fun to visit.

B. Opposite Meanings

Write the spelling words that have the opposite meanings.

14. was ______________
15. does ______________
16. could ______________
17. should ______________
18. do ______________
19. would ______________
20. did ______________

Name ______________________________

A. Circle the misspelled words in the passage. Write the words correctly on the lines below.

Taylor and I have been building model airplanes for years. Today wer'e about to fly two that are radio-controlled. We hope that the skies stay clear and the wind does'nt affect their flight. My mother worries about us, but she shoul'dnt. My father comes along with us for safety. Theres a field nearby with plenty of space. There is'nt much that the planes could crash into. We can't wait to watch them take off. Thats the most exciting part of all!

1. ____________ 3. ____________ 5. ____________
2. ____________ 4. ____________ 6. ____________

Writing Activity

B. Imagine that you were the first person to try something new. What would it be? Write a paragraph about your adventure, and use at least four spelling words.

____
____
____
____
____
____
____
____
____
____

Name ______________________________

Look at the words in each set below. One word in each set is spelled correctly. Use a pencil to fill in the circle next to the correct word. Before you begin, look at the sample set of words. Sample A has been done for you. Do Sample B by yourself. When you are sure you know what to do, you may go on with the rest of the page.

Sample A:

Ⓐ she'l
Ⓑ shel'l
Ⓒ she'll
Ⓓ sh'll

Sample B:

Ⓔ havn't
Ⓕ haven't
Ⓖ havent'
Ⓗ hav'ot

1. Ⓐ wel'l Ⓑ we'll Ⓒ w'ill Ⓓ we'ill

2. Ⓔ did'nt Ⓕ di'nt Ⓖ didn't Ⓗ didn'ot

3. Ⓐ that's Ⓑ tha'ts Ⓒ thats' Ⓓ tha'is

4. Ⓔ your're Ⓕ you'r Ⓖ youre' Ⓗ you're

5. Ⓐ I'ave Ⓑ Ih've Ⓒ I've Ⓓ Iv'e

6. Ⓔ dosen't Ⓕ does'nt Ⓖ dosn't Ⓗ doesn't

7. Ⓐ w'ere Ⓑ wer'e Ⓒ we're Ⓓ we'r

8. Ⓔ should'nt Ⓕ shouldn't Ⓖ shoul'nt Ⓗ should't

9. Ⓐ sh'ed Ⓑ she'd Ⓒ shed' Ⓓ sh'd

10. Ⓔ what's Ⓕ wha's Ⓖ wat's Ⓗ wha'ts

11. Ⓐ isnt' Ⓑ isno't Ⓒ is't Ⓓ isn't

12. Ⓔ there's Ⓕ the'res Ⓖ they'res Ⓗ ther'is

13. Ⓐ hee'd Ⓑ hed' Ⓒ he'd Ⓓ h'ed

14. Ⓔ there're Ⓕ they're Ⓖ th'are Ⓗ theyr'e

15. Ⓐ coud'nt Ⓑ could'nt Ⓒ coudn't Ⓓ couldn't

16. Ⓐ youve Ⓑ you've Ⓒ youv'e Ⓓ y'have

17. Ⓔ was'nt Ⓕ wusn't Ⓖ wasno't Ⓗ wasn't

18. Ⓐ w'have Ⓑ wev'e Ⓒ we've Ⓓ w'eve

19. Ⓔ wouldn't Ⓕ woodn't Ⓖ would'nt Ⓗ wood'nt

20. Ⓐ do'nt Ⓑ d'ont Ⓒ d'not Ⓓ don't

Name ____________________

Fold back the paper along the dotted line. Use the blanks to write each word as it is read aloud. When you finish the test, unfold the paper. Use the list at the right to correct any spelling mistakes.

	1. ______	1. dentist
	2. ______	2. jogger
	3. ______	3. fifteen
	4. ______	4. flatter
	5. ______	5. submit
	6. ______	6. mustang
	7. ______	7. absent
	8. ______	8. hollow
	9. ______	9. empire
	10. ______	10. blizzard
	11. ______	11. culture
	12. ______	12. goggles
	13. ______	13. summon
	14. ______	14. champion
	15. ______	15. kennel
	16. ______	16. valley
	17. ______	17. fragment
	18. ______	18. gallop
	19. ______	19. vulture
	20. ______	20. pigment
Review Words	21. ______	21. won't
	22. ______	22. shouldn't
	23. ______	23. we're
Challenge Words	24. ______	24. clammy
	25. ______	25. hammock

Name ______________________________

Using the Word Study Steps

1. LOOK at the word.
2. SAY the word aloud.
3. STUDY the letters in the word.
4. WRITE the word.
5. CHECK the word. Did you spell the word right? If not, go back to step 1.

absent	valley	pigment	blizzard
empire	submit	goggles	fifteen
gallop	dentist	jogger	kennel
summon	champion	mustang	flatter
fragment	hollow	vulture	culture

A. Fill in the missing letters of each word to form a spelling word.

1. ke _____ _____ el
2. cha _____ _____ ion
3. vu _____ _____ ure
4. ho _____ _____ ow
5. a _____ _____ ent
6. mu _____ _____ ang
7. su _____ _____ it
8. fla _____ _____ er
9. e _____ _____ ire
10. go _____ _____ les
11. pi _____ _____ ent
12. fra _____ _____ ent
13. va _____ _____ ey
14. cu _____ _____ ure
15. ga _____ _____ op
16. su _____ _____ on
17. bli _____ _____ ard
18. fi _____ _____ een
19. jo _____ _____ er
20. de _____ _____ ist

B. Use the spelling words above to write a poem of at least 4 lines.

21. ______________________________
22. ______________________________
23. ______________________________
24. ______________________________

Name ____________________

absent	valley	pigment	blizzard
empire	submit	goggles	fifteen
gallop	dentist	jogger	kennel
summon	champion	mustang	flatter
fragment	hollow	vulture	culture

This week's spelling words have double consonants between two vowels. Sort the words according to the spelling pattern for the double consonants between the vowels.

double consonant repeated

1. ____________
2. ____________
3. ____________
4. ____________
5. ____________
6. ____________
7. ____________
8. ____________
9. ____________

double consonants different

1. ____________
2. ____________
3. ____________
4. ____________
5. ____________
6. ____________
7. ____________
8. ____________
9. ____________
10. ____________
11. ____________

Alphabetical Order

Use the lines below to write the spelling words in alphabetical order.

1. ____________
2. ____________
3. ____________
4. ____________
5. ____________
6. ____________
7. ____________
8. ____________
9. ____________
10. ____________
11. ____________
12. ____________
13. ____________
14. ____________
15. ____________
16. ____________
17. ____________
18. ____________
19. ____________
20. ____________

Name ______________________________

absent	valley	pigment	blizzard
empire	submit	goggles	fifteen
gallop	dentist	jogger	kennel
summon	champion	mustang	flatter
fragment	hollow	vulture	culture

We Go Together

Write the spelling word that matches each clue below.

1. snow storm ____________
2. run ____________
3. winner ____________
4. to praise ____________
5. eye protection ____________
6. between mountains ____________
7. dog's home ____________
8. empty inside ____________
9. not here ____________
10. bird of prey ____________
11. small piece ____________
12. color in paint ____________
13. tooth doctor ____________
14. wild horse ____________

Complete the Sentence

Finish each sentence using a spelling word. Use the word box to check your spelling.

15. The ruler took great pride in his ______________.
16. His people would not ______________ to his rule.
17. The Greek ______________ had wonderful art and architecture.
18. My mother runs to stay healthy; she is a ______________.
19. A judge can ______________ you to be in court.
20. There will be ______________ candles on her birthday cake.

Name ______________________________

A. Circle each incorrectly spelled word in this diary entry. Write the words correctly on the lines below.

My grandfather used to be a star athlete. Even though he's over eighty years old now, he's the most fearless joger I know. He runs up and down the vallie in every kind of weather. If it's raining hard outside, he puts on gogles so that he can see. If there's a blizard, he just bundles up in more layers of clothing. Once he went running when it was fiftene below zero! It takes all the energy I can summin to walk to school on a sunny day!

1. ____________ 3. ____________ 5. ____________

2. ____________ 4. ____________ 6. ____________

Writing Activity

B. Write about a time when the weather forced a change in plans. Use four words from the spelling list.

____

____

____

____

____

____

____

____

____

____

____

____

____

Name ______________________________

Look at the words in each set below. One word in each set is spelled correctly. Use a pencil to fill in the circle next to the correct word. Before you begin, look at the sample set of words. Sample A has been done for you. Do Sample B by yourself. When you are sure you know what to do, you may go on with the rest of the page.

Sample A:

Ⓐ umpirre
Ⓑ ummpire
Ⓒ umpyre
● umpire

Sample B:

Ⓔ scalop
Ⓕ scallop
Ⓖ scalllop
Ⓗ scallup

1. Ⓐ abssent Ⓑ absint Ⓒ abbsent Ⓓ absent
2. Ⓔ vallee Ⓕ valley Ⓖ vallie Ⓗ valey
3. Ⓐ pigment Ⓑ pigmint Ⓒ piggment Ⓓ pigmunt
4. Ⓔ blizzard Ⓕ blissard Ⓖ blizard Ⓗ blisard
5. Ⓐ emppire Ⓑ empeir Ⓒ empyre Ⓓ empire
6. Ⓔ submitt Ⓕ submit Ⓖ subnit Ⓗ subbmit
7. Ⓐ goggles Ⓑ gogles Ⓒ ghoggles Ⓓ goggels
8. Ⓔ fivteen Ⓕ fifteen Ⓖ fiftene Ⓗ fiffteen
9. Ⓐ gallup Ⓑ galop Ⓒ ghallop Ⓓ gallop
10. Ⓔ denttist Ⓕ dentisst Ⓖ dentist Ⓗ denntist
11. Ⓐ joger Ⓑ jogger Ⓒ joggerr Ⓓ joggir
12. Ⓔ kennal Ⓕ kennul Ⓖ kennel Ⓗ kennle
13. Ⓐ summun Ⓑ summonn Ⓒ sumon Ⓓ summon
14. Ⓔ champion Ⓕ champyon Ⓖ champeon Ⓗ champiun
15. Ⓐ musttang Ⓑ musstang Ⓒ mustang Ⓓ mustange
16. Ⓔ flater Ⓕ flatter Ⓖ flattur Ⓗ flattar
17. Ⓐ fragment Ⓑ fragmint Ⓒ fragmunt Ⓓ fraggment
18. Ⓔ holow Ⓕ haullow Ⓖ hollo Ⓗ hollow
19. Ⓐ vulture Ⓑ vulchure Ⓒ vultire Ⓓ vulcher
20. Ⓔ culcher Ⓕ culchure Ⓖ culture Ⓗ cullture

Name ______________________________

Fold back the paper along the dotted line. Use the blanks to write each word as it is read aloud. When you finish the test, unfold the paper. Use the list at the right to correct any spelling mistakes.

1. ____________ 1. minus
2. ____________ 2. loser
3. ____________ 3. humor
4. ____________ 4. closet
5. ____________ 5. recent
6. ____________ 6. student
7. ____________ 7. equal
8. ____________ 8. profile
9. ____________ 9. local
10. ____________ 10. comet
11. ____________ 11. vacant
12. ____________ 12. punish
13. ____________ 13. cavern
14. ____________ 14. shiver
15. ____________ 15. decent
16. ____________ 16. linen
17. ____________ 17. legal
18. ____________ 18. panic
19. ____________ 19. smoky
20. ____________ 20. tyrant

Review Words

21. ____________ 21. valley
22. ____________ 22. fifteen
23. ____________ 23. culture

Challenge Words

24. ____________ 24. fatigue
25. ____________ 25. fugitive

Name ____________________

Using the Word Study Steps

1. LOOK at the word.
2. SAY the word aloud.
3. STUDY the letters in the word.
4. WRITE the word.
5. CHECK the word. Did you spell the word right? If not, go back to step 1.

tyrant	profile	smoky	minus	local
equal	linen	legal	loser	decent
humor	closet	comet	punish	vacant
recent	student	shiver	cavern	panic

Find and Circle

A. Where are the spelling words?

l i n e n c j g l e g a l w p x s t u d e n t h u m o r t u h o

b r d c a v e r n e m i n u s b z t p r o f i l e e t l e q u a l

p u n i s h t o m t y r a n t e y y s m o k y u a t r e c e n t

g i s v a c a n t h p a n i c m u c l o c a l b z t s h i v e r

c o m e t h w v l o s e r f t r d e c e n t l o k c l o s e t e r

B. Write the words below as you find them in the puzzle.

1. ________ 6. ________ 11. ________ 16. ________
2. ________ 7. ________ 12. ________ 17. ________
3. ________ 8. ________ 13. ________ 18. ________
4. ________ 9. ________ 14. ________ 19. ________
5. ________ 10. ________ 15. ________ 20. ________

Name ______________________________

tyrant	profile	smoky	minus	local
equal	linen	legal	loser	decent
humor	closet	comet	punish	vacant
recent	student	shiver	cavern	panic

Sort each spelling word by determining if it follows the V/CV pattern or the VC/V pattern. Write each word in the correct column.

V/CV Pattern

1. ____________
2. ____________
3. ____________
4. ____________
5. ____________
6. ____________
7. ____________
8. ____________
9. ____________
10. ____________
11. ____________
12. ____________

VC/V Pattern

13. ____________
14. ____________
15. ____________
16. ____________
17. ____________
18. ____________
19. ____________
20. ____________

Use the spelling words above to help you write a poem of at least 4 lines.

21. ______________________
22. ______________________
23. ______________________
24. ______________________

Name ________________________________

tyrant	profile	smoky	minus	local
equal	linen	legal	loser	decent
humor	closet	comet	punish	vacant
recent	student	shiver	cavern	panic

A. Definitions

Write the spelling word that matches each definition below.

1. bully ________________
2. empty ________________
3. cave ________________
4. one who lost ________________
5. type of cloth ________________
6. place for clothes ________________
7. pupil ________________
8. the same as ________________
9. subtract ________________
10. shake ________________

B. Finish the Sentences

Write the spelling word that best completes each sentence. Use the word box to check your spelling.

11. The teacher will ________________ disruptive students.
12. I was frightened, but I didn't ________________ when I saw the spider.
13. The mayor laughed at him, so he must have had a sense of ________________.
14. If you're looking at his ________________, you're looking at the side of his face.
15. Was that a ________________ event, or did it happen a long time ago?
16. They wondered if fishing in that area was ________________.
17. The cookies burned, so the kitchen was ________________.
18. The ________________ could only be seen with a telescope.
19. The ________________ pond closest to our house was full of ice.
20. The volunteer proved himself to be a ________________ man.

Name ______________________________

A. Circle the misspelled words in this paragraph. Write the words correctly on the lines below.

Derrick felt that his new boss, Mrs. Pollins, was a more desent person than his old boss, Mr. Flint. His old boss was more like a tierant who didn't care that Derrick was still a stoodent with homework to do after school. Derrick liked working at the locall mall. Even so, he didn't like it when Mr. Flint would punnish him when he took time off to study. Mrs. Pollins had a better sense of huemor and let Derrick adjust his schedule as needed.

1. ____________ 3. ____________ 5. ____________

2. ____________ 4. ____________ 6. ____________

B. Writing Activity

Think about something that you like to do. Has there ever been a time when you couldn't do it and you had to ask someone to help you? Write about what happened, or what you think might happen, in this situation. Use four spelling words.

Name ______________________________

Look at the words in each set below. One word in each set is spelled correctly. Use a pencil to fill in the circle next to the correct word. Before you begin, look at the sample set of words. Sample A has been done for you. Do Sample B by yourself. When you are sure you know what to do, you may go on with the rest of the page.

Sample A:
Ⓐ regu
Ⓑ regal
Ⓒ reagel
Ⓓ reagal

Sample B:
Ⓔ closee
Ⓕ closser
Ⓖ cloeser
Ⓗ closer

1. Ⓐ tyrunt Ⓑ tyrent Ⓒ tirant Ⓓ tyrant

2. Ⓔ profyle Ⓕ proffile Ⓖ profile Ⓗ profille

3. Ⓐ smoky Ⓑ smmoky Ⓒ smokky Ⓓ smokkey

4. Ⓔ mihnus Ⓕ minus Ⓖ minis Ⓗ mineus

5. Ⓐ local Ⓑ lockal Ⓒ locul Ⓓ locel

6. Ⓔ equel Ⓕ equul Ⓖ equal Ⓗ equall

7. Ⓐ linnen Ⓑ linen Ⓒ lynen Ⓓ lynnen

8. Ⓔ legal Ⓕ legul Ⓖ legall Ⓗ leegal

9. Ⓐ lozer Ⓑ loozer Ⓒ loseer Ⓓ loser

10. Ⓔ decent Ⓕ deesent Ⓖ desent Ⓗ descint

11. Ⓐ houmor Ⓑ huemor Ⓒ humor Ⓓ humer

12. Ⓔ closset Ⓕ closet Ⓖ clozet Ⓗ closett

13. Ⓐ comet Ⓑ commet Ⓒ comit Ⓓ comett

14. Ⓔ punissh Ⓕ punnish Ⓖ punish Ⓗ puhnish

15. Ⓐ vacent Ⓑ vaceant Ⓒ vaccant Ⓓ vacant

16. Ⓔ recent Ⓕ rescent Ⓖ ricent Ⓗ resint

17. Ⓐ student Ⓑ stoodent Ⓒ studint Ⓓ studdent

18. Ⓔ shivver Ⓕ schiver Ⓖ shiver Ⓗ shivur

19. Ⓐ cavirn Ⓑ cavurn Ⓒ cavern Ⓓ cavvern

20. Ⓔ pannick Ⓕ pannic Ⓖ panick Ⓗ panic

Name ________________________________

Fold back the paper along the dotted line. Use the blanks to write each word as it is read aloud. When you finish the test, unfold the paper. Use the list at the right to correct any spelling mistakes.

	1. ____________	1. video
	2. ____________	2. poet
	3. ____________	3. riot
	4. ____________	4. piano
	5. ____________	5. diary
	6. ____________	6. radio
	7. ____________	7. ideas
	8. ____________	8. ruin
	9. ____________	9. diet
	10. ____________	10. patriot
	11. ____________	11. fluid
	12. ____________	12. rodeo
	13. ____________	13. cruel
	14. ____________	14. genuine
	15. ____________	15. casual
	16. ____________	16. trial
	17. ____________	17. fuel
	18. ____________	18. meteor
	19. ____________	19. diameter
	20. ____________	20. meander
Review Words	21. ____________	21. recent
	22. ____________	22. closet
	23. ____________	23. minus
Challenge Words	24. ____________	24. situation
	25. ____________	25. variety

Name ____

Practice

Spelling: Words with Open Syllables (V/V)

Using the Word Study Steps

1. LOOK at the word.
2. SAY the word aloud.
3. STUDY the letters in the word.
4. WRITE the word.
5. CHECK the word. Did you spell the word right? If not, go back to step 1.

ideas	piano	fuel	casual	meander
poet	diary	rodeo	trial	genuine
riot	radio	meteor	diet	diameter
video	fluid	cruel	ruin	patriot

A. Fill-Ins

Fill in the missing letters of each word to form a spelling word.

1. cas ____ ____ l
2. rod ____ ____
3. rad ____ ____
4. p ____ ____ t
5. d ____ ____ meter
6. r ____ ____ n
7. vid ____ ____
8. p ____ ____ no
9. cr ____ ____ l
10. met ____ ____ r
11. gen ____ ____ ne
12. fl ____ ____ d
13. d ____ ____ ry
14. id ____ ____ s
15. patr ____ ____ t
16. f ____ ____ l
17. d ____ ____ t
18. r ____ ____ t
19. tr ____ ____ l
20. m ____ ____ nder

B. Reverse Alphabetical Order

Use the lines below to write the spelling words in reverse alphabetical order.

1. ____________ 6. ____________ 11. ____________ 16. ____________
2. ____________ 7. ____________ 12. ____________ 17. ____________
3. ____________ 8. ____________ 13. ____________ 18. ____________
4. ____________ 9. ____________ 14. ____________ 19. ____________
5. ____________ 10. ____________ 15. ____________ 20. ____________

Name ______________________________

ideas	piano	fuel	casual	meander
poet	diary	rodeo	trial	genuine
riot	radio	meteor	diet	diameter
video	fluid	cruel	ruin	patriot

Sort each spelling word by finding the sound and spelling pattern to which it belongs.

ea

1. ______________
2. ______________

eo

3. ______________
4. ______________
5. ______________

ia

6. ______________
7. ______________
8. ______________
9. ______________

ie

10. ______________

io

11. ______________
12. ______________
13. ______________

oe

14. ______________

ua

15. ______________

ue

16. ______________
17. ______________

ui

18. ______________
19. ______________
20. ______________

Name ______________________________

ideas	piano	fuel	casual	meander
poet	diary	rodeo	trial	genuine
riot	radio	meteor	diet	diameter
video	fluid	cruel	ruin	patriot

A. Fill in the Blank

Write the spelling word that best completes each sentence. Use the word box to check your spelling.

1. My sister wrote in her ______________ each day.
2. Did you watch the ______________ about mythical animals?
3. She played the ______________ while he sang.
4. Did all the angry people cause a ______________?
5. Her ______________ included a suggestion for serving better food.
6. I'd like to write a poem about her, but I am not a ______________.
7. We saw horses and cowboys at the ______________.
8. My father went on a ______________ to lose weight.
9. We stopped the ______________. boy from hurting the animals.
10. We wore ______________ clothing because we were sitting on the ground.

B. Definitions

Write the spelling word that matches each definition below.

11. device that plays music and news ______________
12. real, not fake ______________
13. line through the center of a circle ______________
14. move or walk slowly ______________
15. one who supports his or her country ______________
16. rock from space ______________
17. type of energy, such as gasoline ______________
18. destroy ______________
19. decision process in a court ______________
20. liquid ______________

Name ____________________

A. Circle the misspelled words in the passage. Write the words correctly on the lines below.

My friend Ken wants to be a famous poete. He has a genuwine talent with words. He has even written some songs with my sister. She plays the peano and composes music. They even made a vidio of one of their most recent songs. They hope it will be played on the television and raydio some day. They're full of creative ideus!

1. ____________ 3. ____________ 5. ____________
2. ____________ 4. ____________ 6. ____________

B. Writing Activity

What kinds of creative projects interest you? Use the lines below to write about them. Include four spelling words.

Name ______________________________

Look at the words in each set below. One word in each set is spelled correctly. Use a pencil to fill in the circle next to the correct word. Before you begin, look at the sample set of words. Sample A has been done for you. Do Sample B by yourself. When you are sure you know what to do, you may go on with the rest of the page.

Sample A:

- Ⓐ dial
- Ⓑ diul
- Ⓒ dieal
- Ⓓ diel

Sample B:

- Ⓔ audieo
- Ⓕ audio
- Ⓖ audeo
- Ⓗ auddio

1. Ⓐ ideas Ⓑ idees Ⓒ ideaz Ⓓ iddeas
2. Ⓔ poett Ⓕ poete Ⓖ poet Ⓗ poette
3. Ⓐ ryot Ⓑ riot Ⓒ riott Ⓓ rhiot
4. Ⓔ viddeo Ⓕ vidio Ⓖ vidieo Ⓗ video
5. Ⓐ piano Ⓑ pianno Ⓒ peano Ⓓ peanno
6. Ⓔ diery Ⓕ dieary Ⓖ diary Ⓗ dyary
7. Ⓐ radio Ⓑ radeo Ⓒ radieo Ⓓ raidio
8. Ⓔ flewid Ⓕ flued Ⓖ flooid Ⓗ fluid
9. Ⓐ jenuine Ⓑ genuine Ⓒ genuin Ⓓ genuinne
10. Ⓔ rodeo Ⓕ rodio Ⓖ rodeio Ⓗ roddeo
11. Ⓐ meteur Ⓑ meeteor Ⓒ meteor Ⓓ metior
12. Ⓔ crewl Ⓕ crule Ⓖ cruel Ⓗ cruell
13. Ⓐ casual Ⓑ cassual Ⓒ casuall Ⓓ cazual
14. Ⓔ meandir Ⓕ meannder Ⓖ meander Ⓗ meandar
15. Ⓐ diammeter Ⓑ dyameter Ⓒ dieameter Ⓓ diameter
16. Ⓔ fuel Ⓕ fuell Ⓖ fule Ⓗ fewl
17. Ⓐ paitriot Ⓑ patriot Ⓒ paytriot Ⓓ patriet
18. Ⓔ rhuin Ⓕ ruine Ⓖ ruin Ⓗ rooin
19. Ⓐ diet Ⓑ diete Ⓒ diett Ⓓ dyet
20. Ⓔ triel Ⓕ trial Ⓖ triall Ⓗ tryal

Name ______________________________

Fold back the paper along the dotted line. Use the blanks to write each word as it is read aloud. When you finish the test, unfold the paper. Use the list at the right to correct any spelling mistakes.

1. ____________ 1. appoint
2. ____________ 2. laughter
3. ____________ 3. footprint
4. ____________ 4. coastal
5. ____________ 5. bleachers
6. ____________ 6. grownup
7. ____________ 7. encounter
8. ____________ 8. fairground
9. ____________ 9. grouchy
10. ____________ 10. flawless
11. ____________ 11. applause
12. ____________ 12. lawyer
13. ____________ 13. entertain
14. ____________ 14. faucet
15. ____________ 15. caution
16. ____________ 16. boundary
17. ____________ 17. doubting
18. ____________ 18. southern
19. ____________ 19. roughness
20. ____________ 20. although

Review Words

21. ____________ 21. poet
22. ____________ 22. radio
23. ____________ 23. fuel

Challenge Words

24. ____________ 24. nowadays
25. ____________ 25. distraught

Name ____

Using the Word Study Steps

1. LOOK at the word.
2. SAY the word aloud.
3. STUDY the letters in the word.
4. WRITE the word.
5. CHECK the word.
   Did you spell the word right?
   If not, go back to step 1.

footprint	appoint	encounter	entertain	faucet
fairground	coastal	grouchy	applause	doubting
although	bleachers	flawless	boundary	lawyer
laughter	grownup	southern	caution	roughness

A. Fill in the missing letters of each word to form a spelling word.

1. l___ ___yer
2. gr___ ___chy
3. r___ ___ghness
4. appl___ ___se
5. f___ ___tprint
6. entert___ ___n
7. c___ ___stal
8. b___ ___ndary
9. gr___ ___nup
10. l___ ___ghter
11. f___ ___cet
12. c___ ___tion
13. alth___ ___gh
14. enc___ ___nter
15. app___ ___nt
16. fl___ ___less
17. bl___ ___chers
18. f___ ___rground
19. d___ ___bting
20. s___ ___thern

B. Use the lines below to write the spelling words in alphabetical order.

1. ____________	6. ____________	11. ____________	16. ____________
2. ____________	7. ____________	12. ____________	17. ____________
3. ____________	8. ____________	13. ____________	18. ____________
4. ____________	9. ____________	14. ____________	19. ____________
5. ____________	10. ____________	15. ____________	20. ____________

Name ______________________________

footprint	appoint	encounter	entertain	faucet
fairground	coastal	grouchy	applause	doubting
although	bleachers	flawless	boundary	lawyer
laughter	grownup	southern	caution	roughness

Sort each spelling word by finding the spelling pattern to which it belongs.

ea

1. ____________

ou

2. ____________
3. ____________
4. ____________
5. ____________
6. ____________
7. ____________
8. ____________
9. ____________

ai

10. ____________
11. ____________

oa

12. ____________

aw

13. ____________
14. ____________

au

15. ____________
16. ____________
17. ____________
18. ____________

oo

19. ____________

oi

20. ____________

ow

21. ____________

Name ______________________________

footprint	appoint	encounter	entertain	faucet
fairground	coastal	grouchy	applause	doubting
although	bleachers	flawless	boundary	lawyer
laughter	grownup	southern	caution	roughness

A. Definitions

Write the spelling word that matches each definition.

1. a mark left in soft ground ______________
2. near the ocean ______________
3. attorney ______________
4. in the south ______________
5. part of a sink ______________
6. seats at a sports event ______________
7. dividing line ______________
8. select for a job ______________
9. bumpiness ______________

B. Finish the Sentences

Write the spelling word that best completes each sentence. Use the word box to check your spelling.

10. Storytellers who tell tales ______________ their audiences.
11. If the tale is really funny, you hear a lot of ______________.
12. After each performance, you can hear ______________.
13. Some tales have ______________, sly characters in them.
14. ______________ they are tricky, they are often likeable, too.
15. Some of them don't show______________ when they act.
16. As a result, they ______________ problems.
17. You might find yourself ______________ their cleverness.
18. When I am a ______________, I want to tell tales.
19. I will get experience at the local ______________.
20. I hope my storytelling will be ______________.

Name ______________________________

A. Circle the misspelled words in the passage. Write the words correctly on the lines below.

Each year, storytellers from around the United States come to the suothern state of Tennessee for the National Storytelling Festival. Storytellers perform in giant tents and entertane audiences who sit in bleechers. These are the best storytellers in the country, and the tales they tell are flauless. Delighted audiences fill the tents with lafter and applaus.

1. ______________ 3. ______________ 5. ______________

2. ______________ 4. ______________ 6. ______________

B. Writing Activity

Suppose that you were asked to tell a story in a storytelling festival. What story would you tell? Write a story, using four spelling words.

Name ______________________________

Look at the words in each set below. One word in each set is spelled correctly. Use a pencil to fill in the circle next to the correct word. Before you begin, look at the sample set of words. Sample A has been done for you. Do Sample B by yourself. When you are sure you know what to do, you may go on with the rest of the page.

Sample A:

Ⓐ rainy
Ⓑ raney
Ⓒ rainee
Ⓓ rainey

Sample B:

Ⓔ notbook
Ⓕ notebook
Ⓖ noteboock
Ⓗ noatbook

1. Ⓐ lauyer Ⓑ lawyer Ⓒ loiyer Ⓓ loyer

2. Ⓔ uhpoint Ⓕ apoint Ⓖ appoint Ⓗ uppoint

3. Ⓐ cawshun Ⓑ caushen Ⓒ cawtion Ⓓ caution

4. Ⓔ bleechers Ⓕ bleachers Ⓖ bleetures Ⓗ bleatures

5. Ⓐ roufness Ⓑ rouffness Ⓒ rouphness Ⓓ roughness

6. Ⓔ groachy Ⓕ growchy Ⓖ grouchee Ⓗ grouchy

7. Ⓐ incounter Ⓑ incownter Ⓒ encownter Ⓓ encounter

8. Ⓔ fairground Ⓕ fareground Ⓖ fairgrownd Ⓗ faregrownd

9. Ⓐ lafter Ⓑ lauphter Ⓒ laughter Ⓓ laghter

10. Ⓔ aplause Ⓕ applause Ⓖ aplawse Ⓗ applawse

11. Ⓐ footprint Ⓑ foutprint Ⓒ footprinte Ⓓ foutprinte

12. Ⓔ douting Ⓕ doubting Ⓖ dowting Ⓗ dowbting

13. Ⓐ flawless Ⓑ flauless Ⓒ flawliss Ⓓ flauliss

14. Ⓔ costal Ⓕ cowstal Ⓖ coastal Ⓗ coastel

15. Ⓐ bowndry Ⓑ boundry Ⓒ bowndary Ⓓ boundary

16. Ⓔ althow Ⓕ although Ⓖ althogh Ⓗ allthough

17. Ⓐ faucet Ⓑ fauset Ⓒ faucette Ⓓ fausit

18. Ⓔ entertean Ⓕ entertan Ⓖ entertane Ⓗ entertain

19. Ⓐ suthern Ⓑ sauthern Ⓒ southern Ⓓ southen

20. Ⓔ gronup Ⓕ grownup Ⓖ groanup Ⓗ groonup

Name ______________________________

Fold back the paper along the dotted line. Use the blanks to write each word as it is read aloud. When you finish the test, unfold the paper. Use the list at the right to correct any spelling mistakes.

1. ________ 1. stable
2. ________ 2. saddle
3. ________ 3. table
4. ________ 4. noble
5. ________ 5. cattle
6. ________ 6. stumble
7. ________ 7. terrible
8. ________ 8. beetle
9. ________ 9. kettle
10. ________ 10. eagle
11. ________ 11. royal
12. ________ 12. cripple
13. ________ 13. hospital
14. ________ 14. legal
15. ________ 15. label
16. ________ 16. vocal
17. ________ 17. journal
18. ________ 18. medal
19. ________ 19. several
20. ________ 20. sample

Review Words

21. ________ 21. entertain
22. ________ 22. encounter
23. ________ 23. southern

Challenge Words

24. ________ 24. impossible
25. ________ 25. people

Name ____________________

Using the Word Study Steps

1. LOOK at the word.
2. SAY the word aloud.
3. STUDY the letters in the word.
4. WRITE the word.
5. CHECK the word.
   Did you spell the word right?
   If not, go back to step 1.

stable	eagle	terrible	vocal	stumble
saddle	royal	beetle	sample	kettle
table	cripple	legal	noble	medal
cattle	hospital	label	journal	several

Fill-Ins

Fill in the missing letters of each word to form a spelling word.

1. stum ___ ___ ___
2. roy ___ ___
3. ket ___ ___ ___
4. hospi ___ ___ ___
5. sam ___ ___ ___
6. cat ___ ___ ___
7. crip ___ ___ ___
8. nob ___ ___
9. tab ___ ___
10. eag ___ ___
11. journ ___ ___
12. beet ___ ___
13. sad ___ ___ ___
14. med ___ ___
15. stab ___ ___
16. leg ___ ___
17. sever ___ ___
18. terrib ___ ___
19. voc ___ ___
20. lab ___ ___

Name ____________________

stable	eagle	terrible	vocal	stumble
saddle	royal	beetle	sample	kettle
table	cripple	legal	noble	medal
cattle	hospital	label	journal	several

Sort each spelling word by finding the spelling pattern to which it belongs.

-ble

1. ____________________
2. ____________________
3. ____________________
4. ____________________
5. ____________________

-tle

6. ____________________
7. ____________________
8. ____________________

-dle

9. ____________________

-gle

10. ____________________

-al

11. ____________________
12. ____________________
13. ____________________
14. ____________________
15. ____________________
16. ____________________
17. ____________________

-ple

18. ____________________
19. ____________________

-el

20. ____________________

Name ______________________________

stable	eagle	terrible	vocal	stumble
saddle	royal	beetle	sample	kettle
table	cripple	legal	noble	medal
cattle	hospital	label	journal	several

A. Related Words

Write the spelling word that is related to each set of words.

1. ant, fly, ______________
2. robin, hawk, ______________
3. taste, try, ______________
4. award, prize, ______________
5. loud, noisy, ______________
6. tag, sticker, ______________
7. lawful, allowed, ______________
8. kingly, queenly, ______________
9. aristocrat, duke, ______________

B. Fill in the Blank

Write the spelling word that best completes each sentence. Use the word box to check spelling.

10. Yesterday, I faced ______________ challenges.
11. I went to get my horse from the ______________.
12. I put the ______________ on my horse and started to ride.
13. All of a sudden, I felt my horse ______________.
14. I took a ______________ tumble off my horse.
15. I ended up at the ______________.
16. My broken leg will ______________ me for a while.
17. It will make caring for my ______________ a real challenge!
18. Last night, I tried to write about my day in my ______________.
19. It was a challenge just to sit at the ______________.
20. I even needed help putting the ______________ on to make tea.

Name ____________________

A. Circle the misspelled words in this passage. Write the words correctly on the lines below.

Out in the barn, Eli found a leather bag. Inside was an old book. On the cover was a lable: "Abe Jefferson, 1924." Eli could see that it was a jurnle that had belonged to his great-grandfather when he was just a boy. Eli read the first entry: "This morning, I put the sadell on Lightning and went out to round up the catel. In the distance, I could hear a terribal crash of thunder. Severall minutes later, I saw the sky turn a greenish yellow. I wondered if a tornado was coming...."

Eli turned the page. The rest of the book was empty. Eli put the journal in the bag and headed back to the house. Maybe his grandmother would know the end of the story.

1. ____________ 3. ____________ 5. ____________

2. ____________ 4. ____________ 6. ____________

B. Writing Activity

Write an ending to the journal entry, using four spelling words.

____

____

____

____

____

____

____

____

____

Name ______________________________________

Look at the words in each set below. One word in each set is spelled correctly. Use a pencil to fill in the circle next to the correct word. Before you begin, look at the sample set of words. Sample A has been done for you. Do Sample B by yourself. When you are sure you know what to do, you may go on with the rest of the page.

Sample A:

Ⓐ cassle
Ⓑ castle
Ⓒ cassel
Ⓓ castel

Sample B:

Ⓔ peepel
Ⓕ peopel
Ⓖ peeple
Ⓗ people

1. Ⓐ vockal Ⓑ vocul Ⓒ vocle Ⓓ vocal
2. Ⓔ cattle Ⓕ cattel Ⓖ cattal Ⓗ cattil
3. Ⓐ eegle Ⓑ eegal Ⓒ eagle Ⓓ eagal
4. Ⓔ hospitil Ⓕ hospital Ⓖ hospitle Ⓗ hosputal
5. Ⓐ stabel Ⓑ stable Ⓒ stabal Ⓓ staibil
6. Ⓔ sevral Ⓕ sevrel Ⓖ several Ⓗ severel
7. Ⓐ terribal Ⓑ terribel Ⓒ terible Ⓓ terrible
8. Ⓔ tabel Ⓕ table Ⓖ taibel Ⓗ tabil
9. Ⓐ kettle Ⓑ ketle Ⓒ kettel Ⓓ keatle
10. Ⓔ stumbel Ⓕ stoumble Ⓖ stumble Ⓗ stumbal
11. Ⓐ label Ⓑ lable Ⓒ laibel Ⓓ labal
12. Ⓔ crippel Ⓕ crippal Ⓖ cripple Ⓗ criple
13. Ⓐ jurnal Ⓑ journal Ⓒ jurnle Ⓓ journle
14. Ⓔ sampil Ⓕ sampal Ⓖ sample Ⓗ sampel
15. Ⓐ sadel Ⓑ saddel Ⓒ sadle Ⓓ saddle
16. Ⓔ nobil Ⓕ nobal Ⓖ nobel Ⓗ noble
17. Ⓐ beetle Ⓑ beetel Ⓒ beatel Ⓓ bietle
18. Ⓔ legle Ⓕ legal Ⓖ leagle Ⓗ leagal
19. Ⓐ roial Ⓑ roile Ⓒ royal Ⓓ royle
20. Ⓔ medle Ⓕ medel Ⓖ medal Ⓗ meddal

Name ______________________

Fold back the paper along the dotted line. Use the blanks to write each word as it is read aloud. When you finish the test, unfold the paper. Use the list at the right to correct any spelling mistakes.

1. ______________ 1. sugar
2. ______________ 2. gentler
3. ______________ 3. scissors
4. ______________ 4. founder
5. ______________ 5. director
6. ______________ 6. scholar
7. ______________ 7. saucer
8. ______________ 8. labor
9. ______________ 9. commander
10. ______________ 10. error
11. ______________ 11. crater
12. ______________ 12. pillar
13. ______________ 13. splendor
14. ______________ 14. peddler
15. ______________ 15. professor
16. ______________ 16. shatter
17. ______________ 17. governor
18. ______________ 18. vapor
19. ______________ 19. equator
20. ______________ 20. soldier

Review Words

21. ______________ 21. terrible
22. ______________ 22. legal
23. ______________ 23. journal

Challenge Words

24. ______________ 24. refrigerator
25. ______________ 25. remainder

Name ______________________________

Practice

Spelling: *r*-Controlled Vowel Syllables

Using the Word Study Steps

1. LOOK at the word.
2. SAY the word aloud.
3. STUDY the letters in the word.
4. WRITE the word.
5. CHECK the word.
   Did you spell the word right?
   If not, go back to step 1.

commander	vapor	professor	founder
gentler	shatter	governor	crater
labor	peddler	splendor	director
error	pillar	sugar	saucer
soldier	scissors	equator	scholar

A. Find and Circle

Find and circle each of the spelling words in this puzzle. Words may read forward, backward, upward, downward, or diagonally.

R	R	E	T	A	R	C	I	P	R	O	F	E	S	S	O	R	S
C	E	E	R	R	O	R	N	B	J	K	H	X	S	G	R	R	R
K	R	D	T	T	N	W	J	V	O	I	M	M	Y	M	O	E	R
O	O	G	N	R	O	D	N	E	L	P	S	S	Z	S	I	V	A
E	B	O	R	A	D	I	R	E	C	T	O	R	S	D	A	R	L
Q	A	V	W	E	M	R	A	G	U	S	J	I	L	P	O	E	O
U	L	E	C	Q	D	M	H	J	C	O	C	O	O	X	O	C	H
A	W	R	R	U	Q	N	O	W	F	S	S	R	R	D	A	U	C
T	T	N	K	Z	X	X	U	C	S	H	A	T	T	E	R	A	S
O	M	O	D	P	S	S	Z	O	G	E	N	T	L	E	R	S	R
R	A	R	P	I	L	L	A	R	F	O	P	E	D	D	L	E	R

B. List the words below as you find them in the puzzle.

1. ____________ 6. ____________ 11. ____________ 16. ____________

2. ____________ 7. ____________ 12. ____________ 17. ____________

3. ____________ 8. ____________ 13. ____________ 18. ____________

4. ____________ 9. ____________ 14. ____________ 19. ____________

5. ____________ 10. ____________ 15. ____________ 20. ____________

Name ______________________________

commander	vapor	professor	founder
gentler	shatter	governor	crater
labor	peddler	splendor	director
error	pillar	sugar	saucer
soldier	scissors	equator	scholar

Sort each spelling word by finding the sound and spelling pattern to which it belongs. Write the spelling words with the /schwa-r/ spelled:

-or

1. ____________ 6. ____________
2. ____________ 7. ____________
3. ____________ 8. ____________
4. ____________ 9. ____________
5. ____________

-er

10. ____________ 14. ____________
11. ____________ 15. ____________
12. ____________ 16. ____________
13. ____________ 17. ____________

-ar

18. ____________
19. ____________
20. ____________

Name ______________________________

commander	vapor	professor	founder
gentler	shatter	governor	crater
labor	peddler	splendor	director
error	pillar	sugar	saucer
soldier	scissors	equator	scholar

A. What's the Word?

Complete each sentence with a spelling word. Use the word box to check your spelling.

1. The artist used ________________ to cut a hole in the board.
2. The cookie recipe requires two cups of ________________.
3. The meteorite left a huge ________________ in the ground.
4. My teacher found only one ________________ in my homework.
5. We were lucky that the ball didn't ________________ the window.
6. The ship's ________________ spoke to his crew on deck.
7. She wished the movers had been ________________ with the glasses.
8. We put milk in a ________________ for the new kitten.
9. My older brother joined the army to become a ________________.
10. The museum has a ________________ from an old Greek monument.

B. Meaning Match

Write the spelling word that matches each clue below.

11. line around the middle of Earth ________________
12. gas ________________
13. hard work ________________
14. person in charge of a project ________________
15. advanced student ________________
16. traveling salesperson ________________

Name ______________________________

A. Circle the misspelled words in the passage. Write the words correctly on the lines below.

Mary and Carla were watching TV when the house shook. They worried that the windows would shattur. Outside, a mysterious vapur filled the air. They walked over to where a small krater had formed in the yard. They found a strange stone marked with a code. They took it to a professer at the local college. He was a skolar who knew about codes. "You've made an eror," he said. "These are just scratches on a meteorite!"

1. ____________ 3. ____________ 5. ____________

2. ____________ 4. ____________ 6. ____________

B. Writing Activity

Write a paragraph about a mystery that needed to be solved. Use four spelling words in your paragraph.

Name ____

Look at the words in each set below. One word in each set is spelled correctly. Use a pencil to fill in the circle next to the correct word. Before you begin, look at the sample set of words. Sample A has been done for you. Do Sample B by yourself. When you are sure you know what to do, you may go on with the rest of the page.

Sample A:

Ⓐ begar
● beggar
Ⓒ beggarr
Ⓓ baggar

Sample B:

Ⓔ actor
Ⓕ acktor
Ⓖ acter
Ⓗ actar

1. Ⓐ directer Ⓑ director Ⓒ directar Ⓓ direcktor

2. Ⓔ shater Ⓕ shatter Ⓖ shattar Ⓗ shattur

3. Ⓐ soldier Ⓑ soldiur Ⓒ soldiar Ⓓ soldierr

4. Ⓔ govenor Ⓕ governer Ⓖ governor Ⓗ govener

5. Ⓐ errar Ⓑ error Ⓒ eror Ⓓ errarr

6. Ⓔ commandder Ⓕ commannder Ⓖ comander Ⓗ commander

7. Ⓐ peddlor Ⓑ peddlar Ⓒ peddler Ⓓ pedler

8. Ⓔ professor Ⓕ professer Ⓖ professur Ⓗ professar

9. Ⓐ piller Ⓑ pilar Ⓒ pillar Ⓓ pillur

10. Ⓔ splender Ⓕ splendor Ⓖ splendar Ⓗ splendur

11. Ⓐ sissors Ⓑ scissors Ⓒ scissers Ⓓ scissurs

12. Ⓔ vapper Ⓕ vappor Ⓖ vaper Ⓗ vapor

13. Ⓐ scolar Ⓑ scholar Ⓒ scholer Ⓓ scholor

14. Ⓔ sugar Ⓕ sugor Ⓖ suger Ⓗ suggar

15. Ⓐ equater Ⓑ equateor Ⓒ equator Ⓓ equatar

16. Ⓔ laber Ⓕ labar Ⓖ labeor Ⓗ labor

17. Ⓐ foundor Ⓑ foundar Ⓒ foundir Ⓓ founder

18. Ⓔ cratear Ⓕ crater Ⓖ cratar Ⓗ crator

19. Ⓐ saucer Ⓑ sauser Ⓒ sauceor Ⓓ saucear

20. Ⓔ gentlor Ⓕ gentlur Ⓖ gentlar Ⓗ gentler

Name ______________________________

Fold back the paper along the dotted line. Use the blanks to write each word as it is read aloud. When you finish the test, unfold the paper. Use the list at the right to correct any spelling mistakes.

	1. ______	1. slogan
	2. ______	2. woolen
	3. ______	3. listen
	4. ______	4. heron
	5. ______	5. frighten
	6. ______	6. lengthen
	7. ______	7. captain
	8. ______	8. mountain
	9. ______	9. sandal
	10. ______	10. signal
	11. ______	11. global
	12. ______	12. bushel
	13. ______	13. marvel
	14. ______	14. barrel
	15. ______	15. practical
	16. ______	16. pretzel
	17. ______	17. fable
	18. ______	18. chuckle
	19. ______	19. angle
	20. ______	20. nozzle
Review Words	21. ______	21. scissors
	22. ______	22. pillar
	23. ______	23. governor
Challenge Words	24. ______	24. dungeon
	25. ______	25. salmon

Name ______________________________

Using the Word Study Steps

1. LOOK at the word.
2. SAY the word aloud.
3. STUDY the letters in the word.
4. WRITE the word.
5. CHECK the word.
   Did you spell the word right?
   If not, go back to step 1.

practical	lengthen	bushel	pretzel
marvel	barrel	nozzle	slogan
chuckle	global	woolen	frighten
sandal	signal	fable	captain
heron	listen	mountain	angle

A. Fill-Ins

Fill in the missing letters of each word to form a spelling word.

1. ang ___ ___
2. her ___ ___
3. length ___ ___
4. marv ___ ___
5. wool ___ ___
6. list ___ ___
7. bush ___ ___
8. sign ___ ___
9. nozz ___ ___
10. practic ___ ___
11. barr ___ ___
12. capt ___ ___ ___
13. fright ___ ___
14. slog ___ ___
15. mount ___ ___ ___
16. pretz ___ ___
17. fab ___ ___
18. glob ___ ___
19. sand ___ ___
20. chuck ___ ___

B. Alphabetical Order

Use the lines below to write the spelling words in alphabetical order.

1. ____________
2. ____________
3. ____________
4. ____________
5. ____________
6. ____________
7. ____________
8. ____________
9. ____________
10. ____________
11. ____________
12. ____________
13. ____________
14. ____________
15. ____________
16. ____________
17. ____________
18. ____________
19. ____________
20. ____________

Name ______________________________

practical	lengthen	bushel	pretzel
marvel	barrel	nozzle	slogan
chuckle	global	woolen	frighten
sandal	signal	fable	captain
heron	listen	mountain	angle

Sort each spelling word by finding the sound and spelling pattern to which it belongs. Write the spelling words with the /schwa-l/ spelled:

-el	*-al*	*-le*
1. ____________	5. ____________	9. ____________
2. ____________	6. ____________	10. ____________
3. ____________	7. ____________	11. ____________
4. ____________	8. ____________	12. ____________

Write the spelling words with the /schwa-n/ spelled:

-on

13. ____________

-an

14. ____________

-en

15. ____________
16. ____________
17. ____________
18. ____________

-ain

19. ____________
20. ____________

Name ______________________________

practical	lengthen	bushel	pretzel
marvel	barrel	nozzle	slogan
chuckle	global	woolen	frighten
sandal	signal	fable	captain
heron	listen	mountain	angle

A. Fill in the Blanks

Complete each sentence with a spelling word. Use the word box to check your spelling.

1. Celia ate her ______________ for an afternoon snack.
2. The ______________ made an announcement over the loudspeaker.
3. The pain in my foot was caused by a stone in my ______________.
4. The traffic ______________ turned red as she crossed the street.
5. The ______________ of cherries cost four dollars at the market.
6. A thin, white ______________ flew across the sky.
7. She knew it was late by looking at the ______________ of the sun.
8. The tailor tried to ______________ the sleeves by half an inch.
9. The man adjusted the ______________ on the hose to wash the car.
10. We use ______________ blankets to keep us warm in winter.

B. Synonyms

Write the spelling word that comes closest in meaning to each word below.

11. worldwide ______________
12. motto ______________
13. story ______________
14. laugh ______________
15. useful ______________
16. scare ______________
17. container ______________
18. wonder ______________

Name ____________________

A. Circle the misspelled words in the passage. Write the words correctly on the lines below.

Juanita was having trouble finding her left sandel. The mountan hike started at three o'clock, and she was running late. She tried to think back to the last time she wore the shoes. "I put them in a practicul place where I wouldn't lose them," she said aloud. All of a sudden, she let out a chuckel. The lost shoe was underneath the wullen blanket by her bed! Tying the last of the straps, she grabbed a pretsel and ran out the door.

1. ____________ 3. ____________ 5. ____________

2. ____________ 4. ____________ 6. ____________

B. Writing Activity

Write a paragraph about a person you know or have read about who faced a challenge. Use four words from your spelling list.

Name ______________________________

Look at the words in each set below. One word in each set is spelled correctly. Use a pencil to fill in the circle next to the correct word. Before you begin, look at the sample set of words. Sample A has been done for you. Do Sample B by yourself. When you are sure you know what to do, you may go on with the rest of the page.

Sample A:

Ⓐ bottel
Ⓑ botle
Ⓒ bottle
Ⓓ bottul

Sample B:

Ⓔ sharpin
Ⓕ sharpun
Ⓖ sharppen
Ⓗ sharpen

1. Ⓐ angul Ⓑ angle Ⓒ angal Ⓓ angull
2. Ⓔ herron Ⓕ heron Ⓖ herun Ⓗ herrun
3. Ⓐ langthen Ⓑ lengthun Ⓒ lengthin Ⓓ lengthen
4. Ⓔ marvell Ⓕ marvul Ⓖ marvel Ⓗ marval
5. Ⓐ woolen Ⓑ woollen Ⓒ woolun Ⓓ woollun
6. Ⓔ listin Ⓕ listun Ⓖ lissen Ⓗ listen
7. Ⓐ bushel Ⓑ bushshel Ⓒ bushul Ⓓ bushell
8. Ⓔ signal Ⓕ signul Ⓖ signall Ⓗ cignal
9. Ⓐ nozzal Ⓑ nozzel Ⓒ nozzle Ⓓ nossle
10. Ⓔ practicul Ⓕ practical Ⓖ practicall Ⓗ practicel
11. Ⓐ barrel Ⓑ barel Ⓒ barrell Ⓓ barral
12. Ⓔ capten Ⓕ captain Ⓖ captin Ⓗ captun
13. Ⓐ frightun Ⓑ friten Ⓒ frighten Ⓓ frightin
14. Ⓔ slogan Ⓕ slogean Ⓖ slowgan Ⓗ slogen
15. Ⓐ mounten Ⓑ mountain Ⓒ mowntain Ⓓ mountan
16. Ⓔ pretsel Ⓕ pretzul Ⓖ pretzle Ⓗ pretzel
17. Ⓐ fable Ⓑ fabel Ⓒ fabull Ⓓ fabill
18. Ⓔ globul Ⓕ globel Ⓖ globle Ⓗ global
19. Ⓐ sandal Ⓑ sandle Ⓒ sandel Ⓓ sandul
20. Ⓔ chuckel Ⓕ chuckle Ⓖ chuckil Ⓗ chuckul

Name ______________________________

Fold back the paper along the dotted line. Use the blanks to write each word as it is read aloud. When you finish the test, unfold the paper. Use the list at the right to correct any spelling mistakes.

	1. ____________	**1.** unusual
	2. ____________	**2.** underwater
	3. ____________	**3.** regain
	4. ____________	**4.** repaired
	5. ____________	**5.** unaware
	6. ____________	**6.** unfriendly
	7. ____________	**7.** unfinished
	8. ____________	**8.** unimportant
	9. ____________	**9.** refreeze
	10. ____________	**10.** replenish
	11. ____________	**11.** reunite
	12. ____________	**12.** rediscover
	13. ____________	**13.** rewrap
	14. ____________	**14.** disconnect
	15. ____________	**15.** discourage
	16. ____________	**16.** dishonest
	17. ____________	**17.** nonspecific
	18. ____________	**18.** misguide
	19. ____________	**19.** overwhelm
	20. ____________	**20.** submerge
Review Words	**21.** ____________	**21.** listen
	22. ____________	**22.** signal
	23. ____________	**23.** fable
Challenge Words	**24.** ____________	**24.** impatiently
	25. ____________	**25.** inaccurate

Name ____

Using the Word Study Steps

1. LOOK at the word.
2. SAY the word aloud.
3. STUDY the letters in the word.
4. WRITE the word.
5. CHECK the word.
   Did you spell the word right?
   If not, go back to step 1.

unusual	repaired	unfriendly	submerge	unimportant
underwater	nonspecific	discourage	unfinished	rediscover
regain	unaware	overwhelm	misguide	dishonest
disconnect	refreeze	replenish	reunite	rewrap

Fill-Ins

Fill in the missing letters of each word to form a spelling word.

1. ___ ___ usual

2. ___ ___ ___ ___ ___ water

3. ___ ___ gain

4. ___ ___ ___ merge

5. ___ ___ aware

6. ___ ___ ___ connect

7. ___ ___ plenish

8. ___ ___ important

9. ___ ___ ___ specific

10. ___ ___ ___ honest

11. ___ ___ unite

12. ___ ___ discover

13. ___ ___ wrap

14. ___ ___ friendly

15. ___ ___ ___ courage

16. ___ ___ finished

17. ___ ___ ___ guide

18. ___ ___ freeze

19. ___ ___ ___ ___ whelm

20. ___ ___ paired

Name ______________________________

unusual	repaired	unfriendly	submerge	unimportant
underwater	nonspecific	discourage	unfinished	rediscover
regain	unaware	overwhelm	misguide	dishonest
disconnect	refreeze	replenish	reunite	rewrap

Sort each spelling word by finding its prefix.

un-

1. ________________

2. ________________

3. ________________

4. ________________

5. ________________

under-

6. ________________

non-

7. ________________

mis-

8. ________________

over-

9. ________________

re-

10. ________________

11. ________________

12. ________________

13. ________________

14. ________________

15. ________________

16. ________________

dis-

17. ________________

18. ________________

19. ________________

sub-

20. ________________

Name ______________________________

unusual	repaired	unfriendly	submerge	unimportant
underwater	nonspecific	discourage	unfinished	rediscover
regain	unaware	overwhelm	misguide	dishonest
disconnect	refreeze	replenish	reunite	rewrap

A. Opposite Meanings

Write the spelling word that has the opposite, or almost opposite, meaning.

1. lose ____________
2. exact ____________
3. broken ____________
4. fasten ____________
5. completed ____________
6. unwrap ____________
7. important ____________
8. forget ____________
9. thaw ____________
10. use up ____________

B. Fill in the Blank

Write the spelling word that best completes each sentence. Use the word box to check your spelling.

11. Our team works together to study ____________ life.
12. Once I saw a walrus slide off a rock and ____________.
13. Did a big wave ____________ it?
14. Did it ____________ with its herd in the water?
15. Our team has studied ____________ fish at the ocean bottom.
16. Some of them seem to be ____________ of us.
17. Others seem to be ____________.
18. That's why we ____________ anyone diving alone.
19. It would be ____________ to say our job isn't dangerous.
20. Don't let me ____________ you, though. I love my job.

Name ______________________________

A. Circle the misspelled words in the passage. Write the words correctly on the lines below.

I know it is unusuall to love water as much as I do. People tell me all the time that they were unawaire I was such a water nut. Sometimes they are even unfreindly about it, telling me I should get my head back on land. I think this is unimportint, because there is so much going on at the underrwater level. Why sit on dry ground when I could submerdge my body and mind and explore this exciting universe?

1. ______________ 3. ______________ 5. ______________
2. ______________ 4. ______________ 6. ______________

B. Writing Activity

Continue writing the story. Use at least four more spelling words.

Name ______________________________

Look at the words in each set below. One word in each set is spelled correctly. Use a pencil to fill in the circle next to the correct word. Before you begin, look at the sample set of words. Sample A has been done for you. Do Sample B by yourself. When you are sure you know what to do, you may go on with the rest of the page.

Sample A:

- Ⓐ reaplaye
- Ⓑ replaye
- Ⓒ reaplay
- Ⓓ replay

Sample B:

- Ⓔ undun
- Ⓕ undone
- Ⓖ uhndun
- Ⓗ uhndone

1. Ⓐ rediscover Ⓑ ridiscover Ⓒ redisscover Ⓓ ridisscover

2. Ⓔ subbmerdge Ⓕ submurge Ⓖ soubmerge Ⓗ submerge

3. Ⓐ unnfriendly Ⓑ unnfrendly Ⓒ unfriendly Ⓓ unfrendly

4. Ⓔ inusual Ⓕ unusual Ⓖ inusial Ⓗ unusial

5. Ⓐ disscouradge Ⓑ disscourage Ⓒ discouradge Ⓓ discourage

6. Ⓔ disconect Ⓕ disconneckt Ⓖ disconnect Ⓗ discunnect

7. Ⓐ riplenish Ⓑ riplenush Ⓒ replenish Ⓓ replenush

8. Ⓔ ripeared Ⓕ repaired Ⓖ ripaired Ⓗ repeared

9. Ⓐ missgide Ⓑ missguide Ⓒ misgide Ⓓ misguide

10. Ⓔ uninportent Ⓕ unimportent Ⓖ unimportant Ⓗ inimportant

11. Ⓐ reunite Ⓑ reyunite Ⓒ riunite Ⓓ riyunite

12. Ⓔ nonspesifick Ⓕ nonspesific Ⓖ nonspecifick Ⓗ nonspecific

13. Ⓐ regane Ⓑ regain Ⓒ regayne Ⓓ rigane

14. Ⓔ undurwater Ⓕ undirwater Ⓖ underwater Ⓗ unwater

15. Ⓐ uhnfinnished Ⓑ uhnfinished Ⓒ unfinnished Ⓓ unfinished

16. Ⓔ unawair Ⓕ uniwair Ⓖ unaware Ⓗ uniware

17. Ⓐ dishonest Ⓑ disonest Ⓒ deshonest Ⓓ dishonist

18. Ⓔ rifrieze Ⓕ rifreeze Ⓖ refrieze Ⓗ refreeze

19. Ⓐ rerap Ⓑ rewrap Ⓒ rewrappe Ⓓ rerappe

20. Ⓔ overwelm Ⓕ ovirwhelm Ⓖ overwhelm Ⓗ overwellm

Name ______________________________

Fold back the paper along the dotted line. Use the blanks to write each word as it is read aloud. When you finish the test, unfold the paper. Use the list at the right to correct any spelling mistakes.

1. ____________ 1. contest
2. ____________ 2. content
3. ____________ 3. protest
4. ____________ 4. combat
5. ____________ 5. permits
6. ____________ 6. rebel
7. ____________ 7. present
8. ____________ 8. insert
9. ____________ 9. desert
10. ____________ 10. subject
11. ____________ 11. minute
12. ____________ 12. compact
13. ____________ 13. conduct
14. ____________ 14. contract
15. ____________ 15. refuse
16. ____________ 16. conflict
17. ____________ 17. research
18. ____________ 18. excuse
19. ____________ 19. entrance
20. ____________ 20. extract

Review Words

21. ____________ 21. unusual
22. ____________ 22. rewrap
23. ____________ 23. dishonest

Challenge Words

24. ____________ 24. effect
25. ____________ 25. affect

Name ______________________________

Using the Word Study Steps

1. LOOK at the word.
2. SAY the word aloud.
3. STUDY the letters in the word.
4. WRITE the word.
5. CHECK the word.
   Did you spell the word right?
   If not, go back to step 1.

refuse	contest	entrance	present
insert	permits	minute	extract
desert	rebel	contract	compact
subject	conduct	research	conflict
combat	excuse	protest	content

A. Find and Circle

Find and circle each of the spelling words in this puzzle. Words may read forward, backward, upward, downward, or diagonally.

C	E	S	U	F	E	R	F	T	T	T	E	M	T	K	E	T	T	E	T	Y	H
O	C	O	M	B	A	T	G	N	S	C	M	F	G	E	R	C	N	C	C	C	S
N	M	I	N	U	T	E	D	E	E	U	H	I	K	E	I	T	A	O	R	I	U
T	Y	P	G	N	Q	A	N	T	T	D	G	V	S	L	R	R	M	A	J	C	B
R	T	S	E	T	N	O	C	N	O	N	B	E	F	A	T	P	E	X	X	H	J
A	T	R	E	S	N	I	F	O	R	O	D	N	N	X	A	S	V	K	I	W	E
C	P	R	E	S	E	N	T	C	P	C	O	C	E	C	E	L	E	B	E	R	C
T	P	E	R	M	I	T	S	W	N	C	E	L	T	R	E	X	C	U	S	E	T

B. List the words below as you find them in the puzzle.

1. ____________ 6. ____________ 11. ____________ 16. ____________
2. ____________ 7. ____________ 12. ____________ 17. ____________
3. ____________ 8. ____________ 13. ____________ 18. ____________
4. ____________ 9. ____________ 14. ____________ 19. ____________
5. ____________ 10. ____________ 15. ____________ 20. ____________

Name ____________________

Practice

Spelling: Homographs

refuse	contest	entrance	present
insert	permits	minute	extract
desert	rebel	contract	compact
subject	conduct	research	conflict
combat	excuse	protest	content

A. Write the spelling words in alphabetical order.

1. ____________ 11. ____________
2. ____________ 12. ____________
3. ____________ 13. ____________
4. ____________ 14. ____________
5. ____________ 15. ____________
6. ____________ 16. ____________
7. ____________ 17. ____________
8. ____________ 18. ____________
9. ____________ 19. ____________
10. ____________ 20. ____________

B. Make a Puzzle

Make up a puzzle of your own using the space on this page. Give it to someone else to solve. Be sure to include at least five spelling words in your puzzle.

Name ______________________________

refuse	contest	entrance	present
insert	permits	minute	extract
desert	rebel	contract	compact
subject	conduct	research	conflict
combat	excuse	protest	content

Where's the accent?

For each of the spelling words above, the meaning varies according to where the accent is placed. Circle the choice that best completes each sentence. The accented syllable is shown in bold.

1. There was a huge ______________ between the two teams. (**con**flict, con**flict**)

2. Scientists were assigned to ______________ the new disease. (**re**search, re**search**)

3. The director held a meeting to ______________ his findings. (**pres**ent, pre**sent**)

4. Washing hands takes one ______________ of your time. (**min**ute, mi**nute**)

5. The reporter tried to ______________ an interview. (**con**duct, con**duct**)

6. You may ______________ to sign the contract. (**re**fuse, re**fuse**)

7. The coach wanted to ______________ the penalty. (**con**test, con**test**)

8. Our town ______________ dogs in the park. (**per**mits, per**mits**)

9. The school nurse spoke on the ______________ of safety. (**sub**ject, sub**ject**)

10. The ______________ of the book differed from the movie. (**con**tent, con**tent**)

Name ____________________

A. Circle the misspelled words in the passage. Write the words correctly on the lines below.

A crowd of people gathered at the entrence to the auditorium. In fifteen minutes, the winner of the speech-writing contesst would be announced. Omar had sent in his entry after months of careful reserch. The subjeckt of his speech was leadership. If he was the winner, he would be asked to preesent the speech to everyone there. "What an honor it would be!" he thought. He would condukt himself with grace and dignity on the stage. The crowd moved. The time had come. Soon he would know if he had won.

1. ____________ 3. ____________ 5. ____________

2. ____________ 4. ____________ 6. ____________

B. Writing Activity

Write a paragraph about a hero or leader in your community. Use four words from your spelling list.

____

____

____

____

____

____

____

____

____

____

____

____

____

Name ______________________________

Look at the words in each set below. One word in each set is spelled correctly. Use a pencil to fill in the circle next to the correct word. Before you begin, look at the sample set of words. Sample A has been done for you. Do Sample B by yourself. When you are sure you know what to do, you may go on with the rest of the page.

Sample A:
- Ⓐ effect
- Ⓑ efect
- Ⓒ iffect
- Ⓓ effekt

Sample B:
- Ⓔ afect
- Ⓕ affect
- Ⓖ afekt
- Ⓗ uffect

1. Ⓐ excuse Ⓑ excusse Ⓒ exxcuse Ⓓ escuse

2. Ⓔ conttest Ⓕ contest Ⓖ conntest Ⓗ connttest

3. Ⓐ conntent Ⓑ content Ⓒ conttent Ⓓ connttent

4. Ⓔ refuze Ⓕ reffuse Ⓖ rifuse Ⓗ refuse

5. Ⓐ proetest Ⓑ prottest Ⓒ protest Ⓓ protestt

6. Ⓔ conduckt Ⓕ condduct Ⓖ conduct Ⓗ connduct

7. Ⓐ subject Ⓑ subgect Ⓒ subbject Ⓓ subjeckt

8. Ⓔ extract Ⓕ exttract Ⓖ exstract Ⓗ extrackt

9. Ⓐ permmits Ⓑ permits Ⓒ permitts Ⓓ purmits

10. Ⓔ inssert Ⓕ incert Ⓖ insert Ⓗ insertt

11. Ⓐ desert Ⓑ desurt Ⓒ dessurt Ⓓ dezert

12. Ⓔ reble Ⓕ rebbel Ⓖ rebel Ⓗ rebble

13. Ⓐ combat Ⓑ combbat Ⓒ combatt Ⓓ commbat

14. Ⓔ confflict Ⓕ conflickt Ⓖ connflict Ⓗ conflict

15. Ⓐ risearch Ⓑ research Ⓒ ressearch Ⓓ resurch

16. Ⓔ compact Ⓕ commpact Ⓖ comppact Ⓗ compactt

17. Ⓐ conttract Ⓑ contractt Ⓒ contract Ⓓ conntract

18. Ⓔ enttrance Ⓕ entrence Ⓖ entrunce Ⓗ entrance

19. Ⓐ present Ⓑ prezent Ⓒ pressent Ⓓ presunt

20. Ⓔ minnute Ⓕ minute Ⓖ minnut Ⓗ minuht

Name ____________________

Fold back the paper along the dotted line. Use the blanks to write each word as it is read aloud. When you finish the test, unfold the paper. Use the list at the right to correct any spelling mistakes.

1. ________ 1. rancher
2. ________ 2. searcher
3. ________ 3. pressure
4. ________ 4. future
5. ________ 5. butcher
6. ________ 6. measure
7. ________ 7. pleasure
8. ________ 8. mixture
9. ________ 9. treasure
10. ________ 10. feature
11. ________ 11. pasture
12. ________ 12. creature
13. ________ 13. lecture
14. ________ 14. gesture
15. ________ 15. nature
16. ________ 16. fracture
17. ________ 17. moisture
18. ________ 18. stretcher
19. ________ 19. legislature
20. ________ 20. azure

Review Words

21. ________ 21. contest
22. ________ 22. desert
23. ________ 23. entrance

Challenge Words

24. ________ 24. miniature
25. ________ 25. disclosure

Name ________________________________

Using the Word Study Steps

1. LOOK at the word.
2. SAY the word aloud.
3. STUDY the letters in the word.
4. WRITE the word.
5. CHECK the word.
   Did you spell the word right?
   If not, go back to step 1.

stretcher	legislature	gesture	butcher
pasture	lecture	fracture	searcher
creature	rancher	nature	pressure
feature	moisture	treasure	mixture
measure	azure	pleasure	future

A. Fill-Ins

Fill in the missing letters of each word to form a spelling word.

1. fu ___ ___ ___ e
2. crea ___ ___ ___ e
3. sear ___ ___ ___ ___
4. fea ___ ___ ___ e
5. frac ___ ___ ___ e
6. ges ___ ___ ___ e
7. legisla ___ ___ ___ e
8. pres ___ ___ ___ e
9. mea ___ ___ ___ e
10. mix ___ ___ ___ e
11. mois ___ ___ ___ e
12. na ___ ___ ___ e
13. pas ___ ___ ___ e
14. plea ___ ___ ___ e
15. a ___ ___ ___ e
16. stret ___ ___ e ___
17. trea ___ ___ ___ e
18. ran ___ ___ e ___
19. but ___ ___ e ___
20. lec ___ ___ ___ e

B. Write the Words

Use the lines below to practice writing the spelling words.

1. ________	6. ________	11. ________	16. ________
2. ________	7. ________	12. ________	17. ________
3. ________	8. ________	13. ________	18. ________
4. ________	9. ________	14. ________	19. ________
5. ________	10. ________	15. ________	20. ________

Name ______________________________

stretcher	legislature	gesture	butcher
pasture	lecture	fracture	searcher
creature	rancher	nature	pressure
feature	moisture	treasure	mixture
measure	azure	pleasure	future

Sort each spelling word by finding the sound and spelling pattern to which it belongs. Write the spelling words with /chər/ spelled:

-ture

1. ____________
2. ____________
3. ____________
4. ____________
5. ____________
6. ____________
7. ____________
8. ____________
9. ____________
10. ____________
11. ____________

-cher

1. ____________
2. ____________
3. ____________
4. ____________

Write the spelling words with /zhər/ spelled:

-sure

1. ____________
2. ____________
3. ____________
4. ____________

-zure

1. ____________

Name ______________________________

stretcher	legislature	gesture	butcher
pasture	lecture	fracture	searcher
creature	rancher	nature	pressure
feature	moisture	treasure	mixture
measure	azure	pleasure	future

A. Fill in the Blanks

Complete each sentence with a spelling word. Use the word box to check your spelling.

1. It's hard not to ______________ when you're excited or nervous.
2. He had a small ______________ in his hand from the fall.
3. The boiling water sent clouds of ______________ into the air.
4. The chef had to ______________ how much salt to add to the soup.
5. There might be a hidden ______________ somewhere on this island.
6. The air ______________ in my bicycle tires was too low.
7. The professor gave a ______________ on the topic of outer space.
8. The ______________ shop was full of people planning to barbecue on the holiday weekend.
9. After the storm cleared, there was a beautiful ______________ sky.
10. The movie had a ______________ of action, drama, and comedy.

B. Definitions

Write the spelling word that has the same, or almost the same, meaning.

11. animal or living thing ______________
12. person who looks for something ______________
13. special attraction ______________
14. law-making body ______________
15. time after the present ______________

Name ________________________________

A. Circle the misspelled words in the passage. Write the words correctly on the lines below.

William walked outside. Something felt different about the world. There wasn't a creechur in sight. There was a strange moistere in the air. The sky had changed from a deep asure to a light red. He felt a mixchure of surprise, fear, and curiosity. "What was nayture up to?" he wondered. Was something fantastic about to happen? Mysteries like this gave him great pleasher, even when they turned out to be just a sunset.

1. ____________ 3. ____________ 5. ____________

2. ____________ 4. ____________ 6. ____________

B. Writing Activity

Write a paragraph about what you would do if you came across something mysterious. Use four words from your spelling list.

____

____

____

____

____

____

____

____

____

____

____

____

____

Name ____________________

Look at the words in each set below. One word in each set is spelled correctly. Use a pencil to fill in the circle next to the correct word. Before you begin, look at the sample set of words. Sample A has been done for you. Do Sample B by yourself. When you are sure you know what to do, you may go on with the rest of the page.

Sample A:

Ⓐ cullcher
Ⓑ culcher
Ⓒ cullture
Ⓓ culture

Sample B:

Ⓔ teechur
Ⓕ teachur
Ⓖ teecher
Ⓗ teacher

1. Ⓐ futur Ⓑ fewture Ⓒ fuchure Ⓓ future

2. Ⓔ creeture Ⓕ creature Ⓖ creture Ⓗ crieture

3. Ⓐ searchar Ⓑ sercher Ⓒ searcher Ⓓ searchur

4. Ⓔ feature Ⓕ feeture Ⓖ feture Ⓗ fieture

5. Ⓐ fracture Ⓑ frackture Ⓒ fracchure Ⓓ fractture

6. Ⓔ gestture Ⓕ gessture Ⓖ gesture Ⓗ gestur

7. Ⓐ legislaturre Ⓑ legislatture Ⓒ leggislature Ⓓ legislature

8. Ⓔ presure Ⓕ pressure Ⓖ presher Ⓗ preshure

9. Ⓐ measure Ⓑ meazure Ⓒ mesure Ⓓ mezhure

10. Ⓔ mixcher Ⓕ micksture Ⓖ mixture Ⓗ mixtture

11. Ⓐ moistturre Ⓑ moisturre Ⓒ moistture Ⓓ moisture

12. Ⓔ naturre Ⓕ natture Ⓖ nachure Ⓗ nature

13. Ⓐ pasture Ⓑ passture Ⓒ pastture Ⓓ pasturre

14. Ⓔ plesure Ⓕ pleasure Ⓖ pleazure Ⓗ pleazhure

15. Ⓐ azurre Ⓑ azzure Ⓒ azure Ⓓ azzurre

16. Ⓔ stretcher Ⓕ stretchur Ⓖ stretchar Ⓗ stretchure

17. Ⓐ tresure Ⓑ treasure Ⓒ tressure Ⓓ trezzure

18. Ⓔ ranchir Ⓕ ranchur Ⓖ ranncher Ⓗ rancher

19. Ⓐ butcher Ⓑ bucher Ⓒ buttcher Ⓓ butcherr

20. Ⓔ leckture Ⓕ lecture Ⓖ lectture Ⓗ lectturre

Name ________________________________

Fold back the paper along the dotted line. Use the blanks to write each word as it is read aloud. When you finish the test, unfold the paper. Use the list at the right to correct any spelling mistakes.

	1. ________	1. distance
	2. ________	2. importance
	3. ________	3. balance
	4. ________	4. attendance
	5. ________	5. absence
	6. ________	6. performance
	7. ________	7. dependence
	8. ________	8. substance
	9. ________	9. disturbance
	10. ________	10. appearance
	11. ________	11. assistance
	12. ________	12. ignorance
	13. ________	13. brilliance
	14. ________	14. ambulance
	15. ________	15. residence
	16. ________	16. radiance
	17. ________	17. resistance
	18. ________	18. reluctance
	19. ________	19. persistence
	20. ________	20. hesitance
Review Words	21. ________	21. creature
	22. ________	22. measure
	23. ________	23. rancher
Challenge Words	24. ________	24. vigilance
	25. ________	25. inference

Name ______________________________

Using the Word Study Steps

1. LOOK at the word.
2. SAY the word aloud.
3. STUDY the letters in the word.
4. WRITE the word.
5. CHECK the word.
   Did you spell the word right?
   If not, go back to step 1.

ambulance	residence	assistance	reluctance
brilliance	dependence	persistence	disturbance
balance	hesitance	ignorance	importance
performance	substance	radiance	resistance
attendance	absence	appearance	distance

A. Fill-Ins

Fill in the missing letters of each word to form a spelling word.

1. ignor ___ ___ ___ e
2. abs ___ ___ ___ e
3. persist ___ ___ ___ e
4. appea ___ ___ ___ ce
5. reluc ___ ___ ___ ce
6. resid ___ ___ ___ e
7. distur ___ ___ ___ ce
8. brill ___ ___ ___ ce
9. ambu ___ ___ ___ ce
10. resis ___ ___ ___ ce
11. dista ___ ___ ___
12. assis ___ a ___ ___ e
13. ba ___ a ___ ___ e
14. rad ___ ___ n ___ e
15. impor ___ ___ n ___ e
16. hesit ___ ___ ___ e
17. depen ___ ___ ___ ce
18. subs ___ ___ n ___ e
19. atten ___ ___ ___ ce
20. perfor ___ ___ n ___ e

B. Use the spelling words above to help you write a poem of at least four lines.

21. ______________________________
22. ______________________________
23. ______________________________
24. ______________________________

Name ____________________

ambulance	residence	assistance	reluctance
brilliance	dependence	persistence	disturbance
balance	hesitance	ignorance	importance
performance	substance	radiance	resistance
attendance	absence	appearance	distance

Sort each spelling word by finding the sound and spelling pattern to which it belongs. Write the spelling words that contain two syllables and are spelled:

-ence

1. ____________________

-ance

2. ____________________
3. ____________________
4. ____________________
5. ____________________

Write the spelling words that contain three syllables and are spelled:

-ence

6. ____________________
7. ____________________
8. ____________________

-ance

9. ____________________
10. ____________________
11. ____________________
12. ____________________
13. ____________________
14. ____________________
15. ____________________
16. ____________________
17. ____________________
18. ____________________
19. ____________________
20. ____________________

Name ______________________________

ambulance	residence	assistance	reluctance
brilliance	dependence	persistence	disturbance
balance	hesitance	ignorance	importance
performance	substance	radiance	resistance
attendance	absence	appearance	distance

A. Definitions

Write the spelling word that has the same, or almost the same, meaning.

1. great intelligence; shininess ____________
2. the need for someone or something ____________
3. something that takes up space ____________
4. the state of being against or opposed to doing something ____________
5. the state of having little or no knowledge ____________
6. the state of feeling unsure or having doubts ____________
7. a glowing quality ____________
8. opposition; a pull in the opposite direction ____________
9. the act of being present ____________
10. a public display or presentation ____________

B. Fill in the Blanks

Complete each sentence with a spelling word. Use the word box to check your spelling.

11. The thief in prison learned the ____________ of being honest.
12. The acrobat was unable to keep her ____________ on the beam.
13. The ____________ to the store was a little more than one mile.
14. After the false fire alarm, the man returned to his ____________.
15. The drivers in the accident were taken away in a(an) ____________.

Name ______________________________

A. Circle the misspelled words in the passage. Write the words correctly on the lines below.

The firefighter drove a distence of five miles to get to the next town. Once she was there, she went straight to the residance of the mayor. She told him about the nearby forest fire and the importence of preparing the town's residents. She asked for their assistince. At first her appearence frightened the people, but they soon agreed to help. They would do what they could to increase the town's resistence to fire.

1. ________________ 3. ________________ 5. ________________

2. ________________ 4. ________________ 6. ________________

B. Writing Activity

Write a paragraph about a time when you or someone you know had to make a quick decision about something. Use four words from your spelling list.

____

____

____

____

____

____

____

____

____

____

____

____

____

Name ______________________________

Look at the words in each set below. One word in each set is spelled correctly. Use a pencil to fill in the circle next to the correct word. Before you begin, look at the sample set of words. Sample A has been done for you. Do Sample B by yourself. When you are sure you know what to do, you may go on with the rest of the page.

Sample A:
- Ⓐ inference
- Ⓑ infurance
- Ⓒ infrence
- Ⓓ infrince

Sample B:
- Ⓔ viggilance
- Ⓕ vigilance
- Ⓖ vigilence
- Ⓗ vigillence

1. Ⓐ ambullance Ⓑ ambbulance Ⓒ ambulence Ⓓ ambulance

2. Ⓔ apearance Ⓕ appearance Ⓖ appeerance Ⓗ appearence

3. Ⓐ assistance Ⓑ asistance Ⓒ assistence Ⓓ assissance

4. Ⓔ attendance Ⓕ atendance Ⓖ attendence Ⓗ attenddance

5. Ⓐ brillience Ⓑ brilliance Ⓒ briliance Ⓓ brilience

6. Ⓔ deppendance Ⓕ deppendence Ⓖ dependance Ⓗ dependence

7. Ⓐ substence Ⓑ substance Ⓒ subbstance Ⓓ substtance

8. Ⓔ dissturbance Ⓕ disturbence Ⓖ disturbance Ⓗ dissturbence

9. Ⓐ balance Ⓑ ballance Ⓒ balence Ⓓ ballence

10. Ⓔ hesitance Ⓕ hesitence Ⓖ hesatance Ⓗ hesatence

11. Ⓐ ignorrance Ⓑ iggnorance Ⓒ ignorence Ⓓ ignorance

12. Ⓔ importtence Ⓕ importence Ⓖ importance Ⓗ importtance

13. Ⓐ performance Ⓑ performence Ⓒ performmance Ⓓ performmence

14. Ⓔ persistance Ⓕ persistence Ⓖ persisstance Ⓗ perssistance

15. Ⓐ raddiance Ⓑ radianse Ⓒ radience Ⓓ radiance

16. Ⓔ resistance Ⓕ resistence Ⓖ ressistance Ⓗ resisstance

17. Ⓐ relluctance Ⓑ reluctance Ⓒ reluctence Ⓓ rellucence

18. Ⓔ abscence Ⓕ abbsence Ⓖ absance Ⓗ absence

19. Ⓐ residence Ⓑ ressidence Ⓒ residance Ⓓ ressidance

20. Ⓔ disstance Ⓕ distence Ⓖ distance Ⓗ disttance

Name ______________________________

Practice

Spelling: Suffixes

Fold back the paper along the dotted line. Use the blanks to write each word as it is read aloud. When you finish the test, unfold the paper. Use the list at the right to correct any spelling mistakes.

	1.	______________	**1.** serious
	2.	______________	**2.** furious
	3.	______________	**3.** eruption
	4.	______________	**4.** destruction
	5.	______________	**5.** direction
	6.	______________	**6.** position
	7.	______________	**7.** forgetful
	8.	______________	**8.** comfortable
	9.	______________	**9.** finally
	10.	______________	**10.** usually
	11.	______________	**11.** apparently
	12.	______________	**12.** completely
	13.	______________	**13.** eventually
	14.	______________	**14.** carefully
	15.	______________	**15.** microscopic
	16.	______________	**16.** allergic
	17.	______________	**17.** scientific
	18.	______________	**18.** safety
	19.	______________	**19.** activity
	20.	______________	**20.** sickness
Review Words	**21.**	______________	**21.** distance
	22.	______________	**22.** ambulance
	23.	______________	**23.** substance
Challenge Words	**24.**	______________	**24.** aquatic
	25.	______________	**25.** mathematics

Name ______________________________

Using the Word Study Steps

1. **LOOK** at the word.
2. **SAY** the word aloud.
3. **STUDY** the letters in the word.
4. **WRITE** the word.
5. **CHECK** the word.
   Did you spell the word right?
   If not, go back to step 1.

serious	finally	destruction	direction	carefully
eruption	microscopic	usually	apparently	position
forgetful	safety	allergic	completely	scientific
comfortable	furious	sickness	activity	eventually

A. Circle the spelling words in this puzzle. Each word appears once. Words may read forward, backward, upward, downward, or diagonally.

E	G	S	F	I	N	A	L	L	Y	M	Q	C	E	Y	H
E	S	I	W	A	C	M	Q	L	I	R	I	U	L	S	S
R	A	C	T	I	V	I	T	Y	C	P	G	E	O	T	E
U	F	A	A	R	D	N	U	I	O	G	T	F	F	E	R
P	E	F	E	R	E	M	F	C	D	E	N	N	L	V	I
T	T	T	E	R	S	I	S	Y	L	G	O	B	T	E	O
I	Y	I	A	K	T	O	L	P	R	I	A	S	C	N	U
O	C	P	W	N	R	L	M	L	T	T	U	I	K	T	S
N	P	E	E	C	U	O	U	C	R	O	G	C	T	U	U
A	E	I	I	F	C	F	E	O	I	R	V	K	I	A	A
E	C	M	E	K	T	R	F	R	E	D	M	N	B	L	L
S	P	R	U	E	I	M	U	L	L	D	V	E	M	L	L
A	A	D	G	D	O	F	L	T	R	P	O	S	E	Y	Y
C	G	R	I	C	N	A	O	P	Y	I	X	S	R	N	H
P	O	S	I	T	I	O	N	K	E	N	Y	G	T	O	D
F	T	Y	C	I	A	E	N	R	M	S	P	I	P	B	M

Name ______________________________

serious	finally	destruction	direction	carefully
eruption	microscopic	usually	apparently	position
forgetful	safety	allergic	completely	scientific
comfortable	furious	sickness	activity	eventually

Sort each spelling word by its suffix.

-tion

1. ____________
2. ____________
3. ____________
4. ____________

-ful

5. ____________
6. ____________

-ic

7. ____________
8. ____________
9. ____________

-able

10. ____________

-ly

11. ____________
12. ____________
13. ____________
14. ____________
15. ____________
16. ____________

-ous

17. ____________
18. ____________

-ty

19. ____________
20. ____________

-ness

21. ____________

Name ______________________________

serious	finally	destruction	direction	carefully
eruption	microscopic	usually	apparently	position
forgetful	safety	allergic	completely	scientific
comfortable	furious	sickness	activity	eventually

A. Definitions

Write the spelling word that matches each definition.

1. angry ______________
2. at last ______________
3. most times ______________
4. not remembering ______________
5. seemingly ______________
6. instruction ______________
7. place ______________
8. relaxed ______________
9. totally ______________
10. not carelessly ______________

B. Finish the Sentences

Write the spelling word that best completes each sentence. Use the word box to check your spelling.

11. Some scientists study ______________ organisms.
12. They collect and record ______________ data.
13. Many people have an ______________ reaction to pollen.
14. The lack of food created a ______________ problem.
15. The volcanic ______________ sent clouds of smoke into the air.
16. The storm caused a lot of ______________ in its path.
17. Jogging is a healthy ______________.
18. Do you know anyone with a critical ______________?
19. We learned about food ______________ in cooking class.
20. Our family may ______________ need to buy another car.

Name ______________________________

A. Circle the misspelled words in the passage. Write the words correctly on the lines below.

Every time I get near flowers, I sneeze. Apperently I'm allerdgic to them. It isn't serrious, but it does limit my favorite activitie—observing plants and animals. Mom says I may eventualy outgrow the problem. I hope so. I want to be comfortible working outside.

1. ____________ 3. ____________ 5. ____________

2. ____________ 4. ____________ 6. ____________

B. Describe something that you would like to study in more detail. How might you do it? Use at least four spelling words in your description.

____
____
____
____
____
____
____
____
____
____
____
____
____
____
____

Name ______________________________________

Practice

Spelling: Suffixes

Look at the words in each set below. One word in each set is spelled correctly. Use a pencil to fill in the circle next to the correct word. Before you begin, look at the sample set of words. Sample A has been done for you. Do Sample B by yourself. When you are sure you know what to do, you may go on with the rest of the page.

Sample A:

Ⓐ playfull
Ⓑ playphul
Ⓒ playful
Ⓓ playfil

Sample B:

Ⓔ action
Ⓕ acshun
Ⓖ actshion
Ⓗ actien

1. Ⓐ carefuly Ⓑ cairfuly Ⓒ carfully Ⓓ carefully

2. Ⓔ fourgetfil Ⓕ fourgetful Ⓖ forgetfil Ⓗ forgetful

3. Ⓐ useually Ⓑ usually Ⓒ usally Ⓓ usaly

4. Ⓔ safety Ⓕ safty Ⓖ safetey Ⓗ saftey

5. Ⓐ furyous Ⓑ furyus Ⓒ furious Ⓓ furius

6. Ⓔ dierection Ⓕ direction Ⓖ direcshun Ⓗ directshin

7. Ⓐ alergic Ⓑ allergick Ⓒ alergick Ⓓ allergic

8. Ⓔ completely Ⓕ completly Ⓖ compleetly Ⓗ compleatly

9. Ⓐ sickniss Ⓑ sickness Ⓒ sicnniss Ⓓ sikness

10. Ⓔ erruption Ⓕ errupshen Ⓖ eruption Ⓗ erupshen

11. Ⓐ comfortable Ⓑ comfortible Ⓒ comfortibel Ⓓ comfortabel

12. Ⓔ sereous Ⓕ serious Ⓖ sereus Ⓗ serius

13. Ⓐ acktivity Ⓑ aktivity Ⓒ activity Ⓓ activety

14. Ⓔ destruckshen Ⓕ destrucktion Ⓖ destrucshen Ⓗ destruction

15. Ⓐ posetion Ⓑ position Ⓒ pozition Ⓓ poesishen

16. Ⓔ finilly Ⓕ finily Ⓖ finally Ⓗ finaly

17. Ⓐ aparintly Ⓑ apparintly Ⓒ aparently Ⓓ apparently

18. Ⓔ scientific Ⓕ sientific Ⓖ scientifick Ⓗ sientifick

19. Ⓐ eventially Ⓑ eventialy Ⓒ eventually Ⓓ eventualy

20. Ⓔ micrascopic Ⓕ microscopic Ⓖ micruscopic Ⓗ micriscopic

Name ______________________________

Fold back the paper along the dotted line. Use the blanks to write each word as it is read aloud. When you finish the test, unfold the paper. Use the list at the right to correct any spelling mistakes.

1. ____________		1. sweet
2. ____________		2. prey
3. ____________		3. peer
4. ____________		4. pole
5. ____________		5. poll
6. ____________		6. pray
7. ____________		7. waste
8. ____________		8. manner
9. ____________		9. current
10. ____________		10. manor
11. ____________		11. pier
12. ____________		12. waist
13. ____________		13. currants
14. ____________		14. presents
15. ____________		15. counsel
16. ____________		16. presence
17. ____________		17. council
18. ____________		18. stationary
19. ____________		19. stationery
20. ____________		20. suite
Review Words 21. ____________		21. eruption
22. ____________		22. forgetful
23. ____________		23. allergic
Challenge Words 24. ____________		24. kernel
25. ____________		25. colonel

Name ______________________________

Using the Word Study Steps

1. LOOK at the word.
2. SAY the word aloud.
3. STUDY the letters in the word.
4. WRITE the word.
5. CHECK the word.
   Did you spell the word right?
   If not, go back to step 1.

poll	council	waist	manor
presents	current	peer	suite
stationary	sweet	manner	currants
counsel	prey	presence	pier
pray	stationery	pole	waste

Fill-Ins

A. Fill in the missing letters of each word to form a spelling word.

1. su___ ___e
2. sw___ ___t
3. p___ ___r
4. p___ ___r
5. cur___en___
6. curr___ ___ts
7. man___ ___r
8. ma___ ___r
9. po___e
10. pol___
11. station___ ___y
12. stati___ ___er___
13. wai___ ___
14. was___ ___
15. pr___ ___
16. pr___ ___
17. prese___ ___s
18. pre___e___c___
19. coun___i___
20. cou___s___l

Make a Puzzle

B. Make up a puzzle of your own. Give it to someone else to solve. Be sure to include at least five spelling words in your puzzle.

Name ______________________________

poll	council	waist	manor
presents	current	peer	suite
stationary	sweet	manner	currants
counsel	prey	presence	pier
pray	stationery	pole	waste

A. Sort each spelling word according to its number of syllables. Then write the words on the lines below.

One syllable

1. ____________
2. ____________
3. ____________
4. ____________
5. ____________
6. ____________
7. ____________
8. ____________
9. ____________
10. ____________

Two syllables

1. ____________
2. ____________
3. ____________
4. ____________
5. ____________
6. ____________
7. ____________
8. ____________

Four syllables

1. ____________
2. ____________

B. Use the spelling words above to help you write a poem of at least 4 lines.

1. ______________________________
2. ______________________________
3. ______________________________
4. ______________________________

Name ___________________________

poll	council	waist	manor
presents	current	peer	suite
stationary	sweet	manner	currants
counsel	prey	presence	pier
pray	stationery	pole	waste

What's the Word?

Complete each sentence with the correct spelling word. Use the word box to check your spelling.

1. Lori used stamps and stickers to make ______________ for writing letters.
2. The fruit was yellow in color and tasted ______________.
3. The firefighter used a wooden ______________ to move the electrical wire.
4. We ate everything on our plates so there wouldn't be any ______________.
5. The hawk thought the mouse would be good ______________.
6. My father watches the news to keep track of ___________ events.
7. Gary looked shorter in the ______________ of older boys.
8. Our town's ______________ will talk about the need for a new playground.
9. Before joining the debate team, Valerie always acted in a shy, quiet ______________.
10. On my father's shoulders, I can ______________ over the fence.

Name ______________________

A. Circle the misspelled words in the passage. Write the words correctly on the lines below.

Clark never exercised, and his mannor of dieting was poor. Luckily, he liked fresh fruits that were not only suite but healthful, too. His favorites were grapes and currents. On his new diet, his waste shrank by two inches. The boys who had teased him before now came and sought his counsil. They all admired how determined he was. People in the neighborhood went out of their way just to be in his presents.

1. ______________ 3. ______________ 5. ______________

2. ______________ 4. ______________ 6. ______________

B. Writing Activity

Write a paragraph about a project that you would like to accomplish. Use four words from your spelling list.

____

____

____

____

____

____

____

____

____

____

____

____

____

____

Name ____

Look at the words in each set below. One word in each set is spelled correctly. Use a pencil to fill in the circle next to the correct word. Before you begin, look at the sample set of words. Sample A has been done for you. Do Sample B by yourself. When you are sure you know what to do, you may go on with the rest of the page.

Sample A:

Ⓐ flowr
Ⓑ flour
Ⓒ flouer
Ⓓ flauer

Sample B:

Ⓔ flower
Ⓕ flowr
Ⓖ flouwer
Ⓗ flowwer

1. Ⓐ suitte Ⓑ suite Ⓒ suete Ⓓ suette

2. Ⓔ sweet Ⓕ swete Ⓖ swet Ⓗ swette

3. Ⓐ peire Ⓑ piere Ⓒ peir Ⓓ pier

4. Ⓔ peer Ⓕ pere Ⓖ perre Ⓗ peere

5. Ⓐ curants Ⓑ currants Ⓒ currannts Ⓓ currantts

6. Ⓔ current Ⓕ curent Ⓖ currennt Ⓗ curennt

7. Ⓐ mannir Ⓑ mannur Ⓒ maner Ⓓ manner

8. Ⓔ mannor Ⓕ manor Ⓖ mannour Ⓗ manur

9. Ⓐ poal Ⓑ pollel Ⓒ pole Ⓓ poel

10. Ⓔ poll Ⓕ pol Ⓖ polle Ⓗ poell

11. Ⓐ stationarry Ⓑ stationary Ⓒ staitionary Ⓓ staytionary

12. Ⓔ stationery Ⓕ staytionery Ⓖ staitionery Ⓗ stationerry

13. Ⓐ wastte Ⓑ wasste Ⓒ waiste Ⓓ waste

14. Ⓔ waist Ⓕ waiset Ⓖ waiste Ⓗ waisst

15. Ⓐ praye Ⓑ prey Ⓒ preye Ⓓ praey

16. Ⓔ prai Ⓕ pray Ⓖ praye Ⓗ praey

17. Ⓐ pressunts Ⓑ presunts Ⓒ pressents Ⓓ presents

18. Ⓔ pressence Ⓕ presence Ⓖ presense Ⓗ presensce

19. Ⓐ counncil Ⓑ council Ⓒ counccil Ⓓ counsil

20. Ⓔ counsel Ⓕ counssel Ⓖ counsell Ⓗ counssell

Name ______________________________

Fold back the paper along the dotted line. Use the blanks to write each word as it is read aloud. When you finish the test, unfold the paper. Use the list at the right to correct any spelling mistakes.

1. ______		1. prewash
2. ______		2. disable
3. ______		3. discolor
4. ______		4. mistaken
5. ______		5. preheats
6. ______		6. mistrust
7. ______		7. incorrect
8. ______		8. disconnect
9. ______		9. preview
10. ______		10. prejudge
11. ______		11. misjudge
12. ______		12. discomfort
13. ______		13. dismount
14. ______		14. misunderstand
15. ______		15. disobey
16. ______		16. dishonest
17. ______		17. injustice
18. ______		18. disapprove
19. ______		19. inexpensive
20. ______		20. indefinite
Review Words 21. ______		21. presence
22. ______		22. stationary
23. ______		23. current
Challenge Words 24. ______		24. prehistoric
25. ______		25. misbehave

Name ______________________________________

Using the Word Study Steps

1. LOOK at the word.
2. SAY the word aloud.
3. STUDY the letters in the word.
4. WRITE the word.
5. CHECK the word.
   Did you spell the word right?
   If not, go back to step 1.

indefinite	disable	incorrect	dismount
preview	misunderstand	disobey	prewash
dishonest	inexpensive	prejudge	mistaken
disapprove	misjudge	discomfort	discolor
injustice	preheats	mistrust	disconnect

A. Find and Circle

Find and circle each of the spelling words in this puzzle. Words may read forward, backward, upward, downward, or diagonally.

D	P	R	E	J	U	D	G	E	S	K	G	I	E	D	D	P	L	H	E
Z	I	E	C	I	T	S	U	J	N	I	L	N	V	E	I	G	U	S	T
I	R	S	E	G	D	U	J	S	I	M	G	C	I	V	S	G	A	A	I
L	I	Z	H	P	R	E	V	I	E	W	B	O	S	O	C	E	S	W	N
D	W	X	D	O	D	I	S	A	B	L	E	R	N	R	O	N	T	E	I
R	H	X	T	N	N	A	Y	C	D	L	F	R	E	P	M	E	A	R	F
Y	D	B	O	O	J	E	C	P	J	R	N	E	P	P	F	K	E	P	E
Y	E	B	O	S	I	D	S	R	E	F	G	C	X	A	O	A	H	M	D
D	I	S	M	O	U	N	T	T	E	N	K	T	E	S	R	T	E	D	N
M	I	S	U	N	D	E	R	S	T	A	N	D	N	I	T	S	R	G	I
T	C	E	N	N	O	C	S	I	D	U	R	N	I	D	U	I	P	K	J
M	I	S	T	R	U	S	T	D	I	S	C	O	L	O	R	M	D	C	A

Name ______________________________

indefinite	disable	incorrect	dismount
preview	misunderstand	disobey	prewash
dishonest	inexpensive	prejudge	mistaken
disapprove	misjudge	discomfort	discolor
injustice	preheats	mistrust	disconnect

Sort each spelling word according to its prefix. Then write the words on the lines below.

dis-

1. ____________
2. ____________
3. ____________
4. ____________
5. ____________
6. ____________
7. ____________
8. ____________

in-

1. ____________
2. ____________
3. ____________
4. ____________

mis-

1. ____________
2. ____________
3. ____________
4. ____________

pre-

1. ____________
2. ____________
3. ____________
4. ____________

Name ____________________

indefinite	disable	incorrect	dismount
preview	misunderstand	disobey	prewash
dishonest	inexpensive	prejudge	mistaken
disapprove	misjudge	discomfort	discolor
injustice	preheats	mistrust	disconnect

A. Similar Meanings

Write the spelling word that has the same, or almost the same, meaning.

1. wrong ____________
2. lying ____________
3. unsure; unclear ____________
4. cheap ____________
5. frown on ____________
6. go against the rules ____________
7. stain ____________
8. uneasiness ____________
9. divide ____________
10. get down or get off ____________

B. Fill in the Blanks

Complete each sentence using the correct spelling word. Use the word box to check your spelling.

11. If you think that plants are not important, you are ____________.
12. Since Lewis and Clark had no map, it was easy to ____________ distances.
13. When Clark first saw the ocean, he had a ____________ of what we see today.
14. Joseph Andrews once tried to ____________ the machines that chop down trees.
15. The destruction of our natural environment is a real ____________.
16. We should ____________ anyone who wants to destroy our surroundings.
17. When you ____________ your clothes, you use up more water.
18. His mother ____________ the oven before cooking dinner.

Name ______________________________

A. Circle the misspelled words in the passage. Write the words correctly on the lines below.

Many people are mistakin about what they can do to help protect nature. They think that the destruction of our environment is an injustis, but they don't know how they can help. In fact, there are plenty of easy and inexpencive ways to take action. Some people disobay recycling laws because they don't know any better! You can tell people who litter or pollute that you disaproove. Don't prejuge others, but take some time to learn what you can do to help.

1. ______________ 3. ______________ 5. ______________

2. ______________ 4. ______________ 6. ______________

B. Writing Activity

Write a paragraph about things that you can do to help protect nature in your area. Use four words from your spelling list.

____

____

____

____

____

____

____

____

____

____

____

____

____

Name ______________________________

Look at the words in each set below. One word in each set is spelled correctly. Use a pencil to fill in the circle next to the correct word. Before you begin, look at the sample set of words. Sample A has been done for you. Do Sample B by yourself. When you are sure you know what to do, you may go on with the rest of the page.

Sample A:

Ⓐ misshapp
Ⓑ mishapp
Ⓒ misshap
● Ⓓ mishap

Sample B:

Ⓔ missuse
Ⓕ misuse
Ⓖ misusse
Ⓗ missusse

1. Ⓐ dissaprove Ⓑ disaprove Ⓒ dissapprove Ⓓ disapprove

2. Ⓔ discomfert Ⓕ disscomfort Ⓖ discomfort Ⓗ discommfort

3. Ⓐ dishonnest Ⓑ disshonest Ⓒ dishonest Ⓓ disshonnest

4. Ⓔ dismount Ⓕ dissmount Ⓖ dismmount Ⓗ dissmmount

5. Ⓐ dissobey Ⓑ disobey Ⓒ disobbey Ⓓ dissobbey

6. Ⓔ misstakken Ⓕ mistakken Ⓖ misstaken Ⓗ mistaken

7. Ⓐ mistrust Ⓑ misstrust Ⓒ misttrust Ⓓ mistrustt

8. Ⓔ misundderstand Ⓕ missunderstand Ⓖ misunderstand Ⓗ misundderstand

9. Ⓐ incorect Ⓑ incorrect Ⓒ incorreckt Ⓓ inccorrect

10. Ⓔ prevview Ⓕ prevewe Ⓖ prevew Ⓗ preview

11. Ⓐ preheats Ⓑ preaheats Ⓒ prehheats Ⓓ preheets

12. Ⓔ inexpensive Ⓕ innexpensive Ⓖ inexppensive Ⓗ inexpenssive

13. Ⓐ injjustice Ⓑ injustice Ⓒ injustisce Ⓓ injusstic

14. Ⓔ indefinnite Ⓕ indeffinite Ⓖ inddefinite Ⓗ indefinite

15. Ⓐ disabel Ⓑ dissable Ⓒ disable Ⓓ dissabble

16. Ⓔ discollor Ⓕ disccolor Ⓖ disscolor Ⓗ discolor

17. Ⓐ disconnect Ⓑ disconect Ⓒ disconnecct Ⓓ dissconnect

18. Ⓔ missjudge Ⓕ misjudge Ⓖ misjuge Ⓗ misjudje

19. Ⓐ prejudje Ⓑ prejudge Ⓒ preejudge Ⓓ prejuge

20. Ⓔ prewwash Ⓕ preewash Ⓖ prewash Ⓗ prewassh

Name ________________________________

Fold back the paper along the dotted line. Use the blanks to write each word as it is read aloud. When you finish the test, unfold the paper. Use the list at the right to correct any spelling mistakes.

1. ______________ 1. sadness
2. ______________ 2. gladness
3. ______________ 3. needless
4. ______________ 4. harmless
5. ______________ 5. darkness
6. ______________ 6. fullness
7. ______________ 7. stillness
8. ______________ 8. hopeless
9. ______________ 9. fearless
10. ______________ 10. weakness
11. ______________ 11. bottomless
12. ______________ 12. foolishness
13. ______________ 13. fondness
14. ______________ 14. effortless
15. ______________ 15. meaningless
16. ______________ 16. emptiness
17. ______________ 17. forgiveness
18. ______________ 18. motionless
19. ______________ 19. ceaseless
20. ______________ 20. fierceness

Review Words

21. ______________ 21. disobey
22. ______________ 22. mistrust
23. ______________ 23. preview

Challenge Words

24. ______________ 24. weightlessness
25. ______________ 25. thoughtlessness

Name ______________________________

Using the Word Study Steps

1. LOOK at the word.
2. SAY the word aloud.
3. STUDY the letters in the word.
4. WRITE the word.
5. CHECK the word.
Did you spell the word right?
If not, go back to step 1.

emptiness	fullness	motionless	hopeless
gladness	fierceness	stillness	ceaseless
bottomless	darkness	sadness	weakness
foolishness	effortless	needless	meaningless
harmless	forgiveness	fearless	fondness

Fill-Ins

A. Fill in the missing letters of each word to form a spelling word.

1. bottom___ ___ ___s
2. cease___ ___ ___s
3. dark___ ___ ___s
4. effort___ ___ ___s
5. empt___ ___ ___ss
6. fea___ ___ess
7. fierc___n___ ___s
8. fon___ ___es___
9. fooli___ ___ ___ess
10. forgiv___ ___ess
11. ful___n___ ___s
12. hope___ ___ss
13. gla___ ___ess
14. mean___ng___ ___ss
15. har___ ___ess
16. moti___ ___l___ss
17. need___ ___ss
18. sti___l___e___s
19. sa___n___s___
20. wea___ ___es___

B. Use the spelling words above to write a poem of at least four lines.

____

____

____

____

Name ______________________________

emptiness	fullness	motionless	hopeless
gladness	fierceness	stillness	ceaseless
bottomless	darkness	sadness	weakness
foolishness	effortless	needless	meaningless
harmless	forgiveness	fearless	fondness

Sort each spelling word by its suffix. On the lines below, write the spelling words with the *-less* suffix that have:

two syllables

1. ______________________
2. ______________________
3. ______________________
4. ______________________
5. ______________________

three syllables

6. ______________________
7. ______________________
8. ______________________
9. ______________________

Write the spelling words with the *-ness* suffix that have:

two syllables

10. ______________________
11. ______________________
12. ______________________
13. ______________________
14. ______________________
15. ______________________
16. ______________________
17. ______________________

three syllables

18. ______________________
19. ______________________
20. ______________________

Find the two spelling words that rhyme and write them on the lines below.

21. ______________________ 22. ______________________

Name ______________________

emptiness	fullness	motionless	hopeless
gladness	fierceness	stillness	ceaseless
bottomless	darkness	sadness	weakness
foolishness	effortless	needless	meaningless
harmless	forgiveness	fearless	fondness

A. Definitions

Write the spelling word that comes closest in meaning to the words below.

1. still; not moving ______________
2. impossible; without a chance ______________
3. happiness ______________
4. unafraid ______________
5. not stopping ______________
6. unnecessary ______________
7. the absence of light ______________
8. not requiring energy ______________
9. causing little or no hurt ______________
10. love; affection ______________

B. Fill in the Blanks

Complete the sentences, using the correct spelling word. Use the word box to check your spelling.

11. The boys dug what felt like a ______________ hole.
12. When Don read about the accident, he was filled with ______________.
13. After the storm, there was an eerie ______________ in the air.
14. His language was ______________ to the foreigner, who didn't speak it.
15. John began to appreciate the ______________ of the team.
16. The ______________ of the beach was typical for a cold, rainy day.

Name ________________________________

Proofreading

A. Circle the misspelled words in the passage. Write the words correctly on the lines below.

The campers stood moshunless as the bear cub walked around. Even though it looked harmliss, a bigger bear might be lurking nearby. They knew not to test the fearceness of wild animals. They might pay dearly for such fulishness. Soon the mother bear emerged from the darckness and moved the cub away. When the bears were gone, the campers were filled with gladniss.

1. ______________ 3. ______________ 5. ______________

2. ______________ 4. ______________ 6. ______________

Writing Activity

B. Write a paragraph about what you would do if you faced a challenge in the wilderness. Use four words from your spelling list.

____

____

____

____

____

____

____

____

____

____

____

____

____

Name ______________________________

Look at the words in each set below. One word in each set is spelled correctly. Use a pencil to fill in the circle next to the correct word. Before you begin, look at the sample set of words. Sample A has been done for you. Do Sample B by yourself. When you are sure you know what to do, you may go on with the rest of the page.

Sample A:

Ⓐ useless
Ⓑ usseless
Ⓒ uselless
Ⓓ ueseless

Sample B:

Ⓔ hapyness
Ⓕ happyness
Ⓖ hapiness
Ⓗ happiness

1. Ⓐ botomless Ⓑ bottommless Ⓒ bottomless Ⓓ botommless

2. Ⓔ ceaselless Ⓕ ceasless Ⓖ ceaseless Ⓗ ceeseless

3. Ⓐ darknness Ⓑ darkness Ⓒ darknes Ⓓ darkkness

4. Ⓔ efortlless Ⓕ effortlless Ⓖ efortless Ⓗ effortless

5. Ⓐ emptynness Ⓑ emptinness Ⓒ epmtyness Ⓓ emptiness

6. Ⓔ fearlless Ⓕ fearless Ⓖ feerless Ⓗ fereless

7. Ⓐ fiercenness Ⓑ feirceness Ⓒ fierceness Ⓓ feircenness

8. Ⓔ fonddnness Ⓕ fondnness Ⓖ fonddness Ⓗ fondness

9. Ⓗ foolishness Ⓑ foollishness Ⓒ foolishnness Ⓓ foollishnness

10. Ⓔ forgiveness Ⓕ forggiveness Ⓖ forgivenness Ⓗ foregiveness

11. Ⓐ fullness Ⓑ fulness Ⓒ fullnness Ⓓ fulnness

12. Ⓔ hopelless Ⓕ hopeless Ⓖ hopless Ⓗ hoppeless

13. Ⓐ gladdnness Ⓑ gladnness Ⓒ gladdness Ⓓ gladness

14. Ⓔ meaninglless Ⓕ meanningless Ⓖ meaningless Ⓗ meaninggless

15. Ⓐ harmmless Ⓑ harmless Ⓒ harmlless Ⓓ harrmless

16. Ⓔ motionlless Ⓕ motionnless Ⓖ mottionless Ⓗ motionless

17. Ⓐ needlless Ⓑ needeless Ⓒ needless Ⓓ neadless

18. Ⓔ stillness Ⓕ stilness Ⓖ stillnness Ⓗ stilnness

19. Ⓐ sadnness Ⓑ saddness Ⓒ sadness Ⓓ saddnness

20. Ⓔ weekness Ⓕ weakness Ⓖ weakeness Ⓗ weaknness

Name ____________________

Fold back the paper along the dotted line. Use the blanks to write each word as it is read aloud. When you finish the test, unfold the paper. Use the list at the right to correct any spelling mistakes.

1. ____________ 1. impress
2. ____________ 2. correct
3. ____________ 3. elect
4. ____________ 4. discuss
5. ____________ 5. locate
6. ____________ 6. decorate
7. ____________ 7. confuse
8. ____________ 8. estimate
9. ____________ 9. impression
10. ____________ 10. correction
11. ____________ 11. election
12. ____________ 12. discussion
13. ____________ 13. location
14. ____________ 14. decoration
15. ____________ 15. confusion
16. ____________ 16. estimation
17. ____________ 17. concentrate
18. ____________ 18. exhaust
19. ____________ 19. concentration
20. ____________ 20. exhaustion

Review Words

21. ____________ 21. hopeless
22. ____________ 22. fearless
23. ____________ 23. forgiveness

Challenge Words

24. ____________ 24. conclude
25. ____________ 25. conclusion

Name ____

Using the Word Study Steps

1. LOOK at the word.
2. SAY the word aloud.
3. STUDY the letters in the word.
4. WRITE the word.
5. CHECK the word.
Did you spell the word right?
If not, go back to step 1.

exhaustion	impression	location	elect
decoration	discussion	discuss	correct
election	confuse	estimation	confusion
impress	concentration	correction	concentrate
locate	exhaust	decorate	estimate

Fill-Ins

A. Fill in the missing letters of each word to form a spelling word.

1. disc___ ___s
2. loca___ ___
3. imp___ ___ss
4. el___ ___t
5. elect___ ___n
6. correc___ ___on
7. decor___ ___e
8. confusi___ ___
9. concentrati___ ___
10. concentra___ ___
11. discus___ ___on
12. loca___ ___ ___n
13. impress___ ___ ___
14. corre___ ___
15. confu___ ___
16. decora___ ___on
17. estim___ ___ion
18. exhau___ ___
19. exhaust___ ___ ___
20. estim___ ___e

Name ____________________

exhaustion	impression	location	elect
decoration	discussion	discuss	correct
election	confuse	estimation	confusion
impress	concentration	correction	concentrate
locate	exhaust	decorate	estimate

Sort each spelling word by finding the sound and spelling pattern to which it belongs. Write the spelling words with the ending spelled:

-ate

1. ____________________
2. ____________________
3. ____________________
4. ____________________

-ct

11. ____________________
12. ____________________

-ss

13. ____________________
14. ____________________

Write the spelling words with the ending spelled:

-se

5. ____________________

-st

6. ____________________

-tion

7. ____________________
8. ____________________
9. ____________________
10. ____________________

15. ____________________
16. ____________________
17. ____________________

-sion

18. ____________________
19. ____________________
20. ____________________

Name ______________________________

exhaustion	impression	location	elect
decoration	discussion	discuss	correct
election	confuse	estimation	confusion
impress	concentration	correction	concentrate
locate	exhaust	decorate	estimate

A. Meaning Match

Write the spelling word that matches each clue below.

1. the state of being tired ______________
2. the act of thinking ______________
3. to guess ______________
4. the result of voting ______________
5. to find ______________
6. an opinion ______________
7. to talk ______________
8. to have a strong effect on ______________
9. a place ______________
10. the act of making right ______________

B. Fill in the Blanks

Complete each sentence with a spelling word. Use the word box to check your spelling.

11. When Eleanor works she needs to ______________.
12. At first, there was some ______________ about the who said what.
13. The old car blew ______________ into the air.
14. No one had time to ______________ the room for the party.
15. Our first ______________ was that the movie would be a big hit.
16. They decided to ______________ me for class president.
17. Their ______________ about the news lasted into the night.
18. Irina was ______________ about the number of plates we needed.

Name ______________________________

Proofreading

A. Circle the misspelled words in the passage. Write the words correctly on the lines below.

After driving around in a circle, our father pulled over to consentrate on the map. He figured out our current locashun. No wonder there was confushion! One sign said "First Street" and another said "First Avenue." Father figured out how to corect our course. After some discusion about time, we were on our way. Soon we were able to lokate our destination!

1. ______________ 3. ______________ 5. ______________

2. ______________ 4. ______________ 6. ______________

B. Writing Activity

Write a paragraph about a time when you or a person you know planned a long trip. Use four words from your spelling list.

____

____

____

____

____

____

____

____

____

____

____

____

____

____

Name ____________________

Look at the words in each set below. One word in each set is spelled correctly. Use a pencil to fill in the circle next to the correct word. Before you begin, look at the sample set of words. Sample A has been done for you. Do Sample B by yourself. When you are sure you know what to do, you may go on with the rest of the page.

Sample A:

Ⓐ edditt
Ⓑ eddit
Ⓒ edit
Ⓓ editt

Sample B:

Ⓔ eddition
Ⓕ edition
Ⓖ edittion
Ⓗ eddittion

1. Ⓐ concentrate Ⓑ conncentrate Ⓒ concenntrate Ⓓ concentratte

2. Ⓔ concetration Ⓕ concentration Ⓖ conncetration Ⓗ conncentration

3. Ⓐ confusse Ⓑ connffuse Ⓒ conffuse Ⓓ confuse

4. Ⓔ confusion Ⓕ conffusion Ⓖ confussion Ⓗ conffussion

5. Ⓐ correct Ⓑ corect Ⓒ correckt Ⓓ coreckt

6. Ⓔ corection Ⓕ correction Ⓖ correcktion Ⓗ corecktion

7. Ⓐ deccorrate Ⓑ decorrate Ⓒ deccorate Ⓓ decorate

8. Ⓔ decorration Ⓕ deccoration Ⓖ deccorration Ⓗ decoration

9. Ⓐ ellect Ⓑ elect Ⓒ eleckt Ⓓ elleckt

10. Ⓔ election Ⓕ ellection Ⓖ elecktion Ⓗ ellecktion

11. Ⓐ esttimate Ⓑ esstimate Ⓒ estimmate Ⓓ estimate

12. Ⓔ estimmation Ⓕ esttimmation Ⓖ esttimation Ⓗ estimation

13. Ⓐ exaust Ⓑ exhaust Ⓒ exxhaust Ⓓ exhaustt

14. Ⓔ exaustion Ⓕ exxhaution Ⓖ exhaustion Ⓗ exxaution

15. Ⓐ impress Ⓑ immpress Ⓒ imppress Ⓓ impres

16. Ⓔ imppresion Ⓕ impresion Ⓖ immpression Ⓗ impression

17. Ⓐ locate Ⓑ loccate Ⓒ locatte Ⓓ loccatte

18. Ⓔ loccation Ⓕ location Ⓖ locattion Ⓗ loccattion

19. Ⓐ discusss Ⓑ disscus Ⓒ disscuss Ⓓ discuss

20. Ⓔ discussion Ⓕ discusion Ⓖ disscussion Ⓗ disccussion

Name ____________________

Fold back the paper along the dotted line. Use the blanks to write each word as it is read aloud. When you finish the test, unfold the paper. Use the list at the right to correct any spelling mistakes.

	1. ____________	1. astronaut
	2. ____________	2. telephone
	3. ____________	3. automobile
	4. ____________	4. photography
	5. ____________	5. mechanical
	6. ____________	6. myth
	7. ____________	7. television
	8. ____________	8. phonics
	9. ____________	9. automatic
	10. ____________	10. photograph
	11. ____________	11. telescope
	12. ____________	12. mythical
	13. ____________	13. telegraph
	14. ____________	14. mechanic
	15. ____________	15. telegram
	16. ____________	16. telephoto
	17. ____________	17. autograph
	18. ____________	18. astronomer
	19. ____________	19. disaster
	20. ____________	20. homophone
Review Words	21. ____________	21. correction
	22. ____________	22. discussion
	23. ____________	23. decoration
Challenge Words	24. ____________	24. videophone
	25. ____________	25. photogenic

Name ______________________________

Using the Word Study Steps

1. LOOK at the word.
2. SAY the word aloud.
3. STUDY the letters in the word.
4. WRITE the word.
5. CHECK the word. Did you spell the word right? If not, go back to step 1.

telegram	automatic	homophone	myth
mechanic	disaster	telegraph	astronaut
automobile	telephoto	astronomer	photograph
photography	telescope	autograph	telephone
phonics	mechanical	television	mythical

A. Fill-Ins

Fill in the missing letters of each word to form a spelling word.

1. a ___ t ___ onaut
2. a ___ t ___ graph
3. aut ___ m ___ tic
4. a ___ to ___ ___ bile
5. m ___ ___ hical
6. ___ e ___ egraph
7. t ___ l ___ phone
8. ___ el ___ ___ cope
9. te ___ ___ ___ ision
10. te ___ eg ___ am
11. hom ___ ___ h ___ ne
12. p ___ o ___ ics
13. di ___ a ___ ___ er
14. ___ st ___ ___ nomer
15. p ___ ___ t ___ graph
16. ___ ___ otogr ___ phy
17. m ___ ___ h
18. me ___ ___ an ___ c
19. ___ ec ___ anic ___ l
20. t ___ le ___ ___ oto

B. Make a Puzzle

Make up a puzzle of your own using the space on this page. Give it to someone else to solve. Be sure to include at least five spelling words in your puzzle.

Name ______________________________

telegram	automatic	homophone	myth
mechanic	disaster	telegraph	astronaut
automobile	telephoto	astronomer	photograph
photography	telescope	autograph	telephone
phonics	mechanical	television	mythical

Sort each spelling word according to the Greek root it contains. Then write the words on the lines below. Some words may be placed into more than one category.

astro / ***aster***

1. ______ 2. ______ 3. ______

auto

4. ______ 5. ______ 6. ______

photo

7. ______ 8. ______ 9. ______

tele

10. ______ 11. ______ 12. ______
13. ______ 14. ______ 15. ______

phon

16. ______ 17. ______ 18. ______

mech

19. ______ 20. ______

myth

21. ______ 22. ______

Name ______________________________

telegram	automatic	homophone	myth
mechanic	disaster	telegraph	astronaut
automobile	telephoto	astronomer	photograph
photography	telescope	autograph	telephone
phonics	mechanical	television	mythical

Complete each sentence below with a spelling word. Use the word bank to check your spelling.

1. Tomas gazed up at the stars through his ________________.
2. A ________________ of the bird would have helped us identify it.
3. Clint had no ________________, so he had to ride his bike.
4. The unicorn is a ________________ creature.
5. The word "fair" is a ________________ of "fare."
6. If the flooding continued, it would have been a ________________.
7. The storyteller told a ________________ about how the world was formed.
8. An ________________ showed us where the comet would appear.
9. The inventor designed a ________________ device for tying shoes.
10. The ________________ rang and rang but no answered it.

Write On!

Use each spelling word in a sentence.

11. mechanic ________________________________
12. television ________________________________
13. astronaut ________________________________
14. photography ________________________________
15. autograph ________________________________

Name ____________________

A. Circle the misspelled words in the passage. Write the words correctly on the lines below.

Andrea turned on the telivision. There was a program on about a mithical bird and a horse. She picked up the telefone to call Jill, but no one answered. The automatick answering machine clicked on, and Andrea began to leave a message.

"I was doing my phonicks homework when this show came on!" she exclaimed. "There's a bird on TV that looks just like the one in the photagraph you have. Turn on channel eight, if you're home."

1. ____________ 3. ____________ 5. ____________

2. ____________ 4. ____________ 6. ____________

B. Writing Activity

Write a paragraph about what you would have done if you were Sage. Use four words from your spelling list.

____

____

____

____

____

____

____

____

____

____

____

____

____

Name ______________________________

Practice

Spelling: Words with Greek Roots

Look at the words in each set below. One word in each set is spelled correctly. Use a pencil to fill in the circle next to the correct word. Before you begin, look at the sample set of words. Sample A has been done for you. Do Sample B by yourself. When you are sure you know what to do, you may go on with the rest of the page.

Sample A:

Ⓐ kilometer
Ⓑ killometer
Ⓒ kilommeter
Ⓓ killommeter

Sample B:

Ⓔ phoeton
Ⓕ foton
Ⓖ photton
Ⓗ photon

1. Ⓐ astronat Ⓑ astanaut Ⓒ astronaut Ⓓ astranat
2. Ⓔ autagraph Ⓕ autograph Ⓖ auttograph Ⓗ autograf
3. Ⓐ automattic Ⓑ automatic Ⓒ auttomatic Ⓓ auttomattic
4. Ⓔ autommobile Ⓕ autommobil Ⓖ automobil Ⓗ automobile
5. Ⓐ mythical Ⓑ mythiccal Ⓒ mithical Ⓓ mithiccal
6. Ⓔ telegraph Ⓕ tellegraph Ⓖ telleggraph Ⓗ teleggraph
7. Ⓐ tellepphone Ⓑ telepphone Ⓒ tellephone Ⓓ telephone
8. Ⓔ tellescope Ⓕ telescope Ⓖ telesscope Ⓗ tellesscope
9. Ⓐ tellevision Ⓑ television Ⓒ televission Ⓓ tellevission
10. Ⓔ telegram Ⓕ tellegram Ⓖ telegramm Ⓗ tellegramm
11. Ⓐ homopphone Ⓑ hommophone Ⓒ homophone Ⓓ hommopphone
12. Ⓔ phanics Ⓕ phonix Ⓖ phonnics Ⓗ phonics
13. Ⓐ disaster Ⓑ dissaster Ⓒ disasster Ⓓ dissasster
14. Ⓔ astranomer Ⓕ astronomer Ⓖ astronommer Ⓗ asrtonnomer
15. Ⓐ photograph Ⓑ phottograph Ⓒ photoggraph Ⓓ phottoggraph
16. Ⓔ photoggraphy Ⓕ phottography Ⓖ photagraphy Ⓗ photography
17. Ⓐ mytth Ⓑ mith Ⓒ myth Ⓓ myeth
18. Ⓔ machanic Ⓕ mechanic Ⓖ mecanic Ⓗ macanic
19. Ⓐ mechanical Ⓑ mecanical Ⓒ mechanacal Ⓓ mecanacal
20. Ⓔ telephoto Ⓕ tellephoto Ⓖ telefoto Ⓗ tellefoto

Name ______________________________

Fold back the paper along the dotted line. Use the blanks to write each word as it is read aloud. When you finish the test, unfold the paper. Use the list at the right to correct any spelling mistakes.

1. ______________ 1. subtraction
2. ______________ 2. transportation
3. ______________ 3. missile
4. ______________ 4. portable
5. ______________ 5. export
6. ______________ 6. committee
7. ______________ 7. respect
8. ______________ 8. transport
9. ______________ 9. tractor
10. ______________ 10. spectator
11. ______________ 11. attraction
12. ______________ 12. dismiss
13. ______________ 13. inspector
14. ______________ 14. distract
15. ______________ 15. spectacle
16. ______________ 16. inspect
17. ______________ 17. mission
18. ______________ 18. import
19. ______________ 19. intermission
20. ______________ 20. suspect

Review Words

21. ______________ 21. telescope
22. ______________ 22. astronaut
23. ______________ 23. photograph

Challenge Words

24. ______________ 24. spectacular
25. ______________ 25. protractor

Name ______________________________

Using the Word Study Steps

1. LOOK at the word.
2. SAY the word aloud.
3. STUDY the letters in the word.
4. WRITE the word.
5. CHECK the word.
   Did you spell the word right?
   If not, go back to step 1.

transport	attraction	intermission	portable
spectacle	committee	dismiss	missile
distract	tractor	export	transportation
respect	import	suspect	inspector
spectator	mission	subtraction	inspect

A. Find and Circle

Find and circle each of the spelling words in this puzzle. Words may read forward, backward, upward, or downward.

E	R	E	S	P	E	C	T	S	S	I	M	S	I	D	O	A	A	S	R
L	V	T	R	A	N	S	P	O	R	T	I	M	P	O	R	T	T	P	O
I	H	S	N	O	I	T	A	T	R	O	P	S	N	A	R	T	T	E	T
S	W	M	C	N	E	E	E	T	T	I	M	M	O	C	N	Z	R	C	C
S	N	O	I	S	S	I	M	R	E	T	N	I	T	Y	F	F	A	T	E
I	I	P	D	I	S	T	R	A	C	T	G	N	Q	M	P	R	C	A	P
M	T	P	O	R	T	A	B	L	E	T	C	E	P	S	U	S	T	T	S
E	L	C	A	T	C	E	P	S	T	C	E	P	S	N	I	M	I	O	N
N	O	I	S	S	I	M	R	J	T	R	A	C	T	O	R	J	O	R	I
N	O	I	T	C	A	R	T	B	U	S	T	R	O	P	X	E	N	Z	O

Name ______________________________

transport	attraction	intermission	portable
spectacle	committee	dismiss	missile
distract	tractor	export	transportation
respect	import	suspect	inspector
spectator	mission	subtraction	inspect

Sort each spelling word according to the Latin root it contains. Then write the words on the lines below.

mit/miss

1. ____________ **3.** ____________ **5.** ____________

2. ____________ **4.** ____________

port

6. ____________ **8.** ____________ **10.** ____________

7. ____________ **9.** ____________

spect

11. ____________ **13.** ____________ **15.** ____________

12. ____________ **14.** ____________ **16.** ____________

tract

17. ____________ **19.** ____________

18. ____________ **20.** ____________

Name ______________________________

transport	attraction	intermission	portable
spectacle	committee	dismiss	missile
distract	tractor	export	transportation
respect	import	suspect	inspector
spectator	mission	subtraction	inspect

A. Definitions

Write the spelling word that has the same, or almost the same, meaning. Use the word box to check your spelling.

1. group of people assigned to one task ____________
2. person who finds out information or judges something ____________
3. a task or project ____________
4. to send away; a product that is sent from one country to another ____________
5. able to be moved from one place to another ____________
6. special regard for a person or thing ____________
7. vehicle used for farming ____________
8. the act of removing or taking away ____________
9. a person who witnesses an event ____________
10. to shift attention away from something ____________

B. Fill in the Blanks

Complete each sentence with a spelling word.

11. I ____________ that a picnic is not much fun in the rain.
12. Cars, buses, trucks, and trains are all forms of ____________.
13. Some people like to ____________ their food before they eat it.
14. Do other countries ____________ cars from the United States?
15. We left the play during the ____________ because we were tired.

Name ______________________________

A. Circle the misspelled words in the passage. Write the words correctly on the lines below.

It takes some effort and energy to be a spektater at our school's sporting events. Even though the athletes are the main attracion, we sing songs, hold up signs, and learn loud cheers. Sometimes it can distrack the other team's players. I suspekt that this is why our teams win more often when they play at home. Our main mishun is to boost their spirits. No matter who wins, we treat all the players with the respeckt they deserve.

1. ____________ **3.** ____________ **5.** ____________

2. ____________ **4.** ____________ **6.** ____________

B. Writing Activity

Write a paragraph about a sports activity you would enjoy playing or seeing. Use four words from your spelling list.

Name ______________________________

Look at the words in each set below. One word in each set is spelled correctly. Use a pencil to fill in the circle next to the correct word. Before you begin, look at the sample set of words. Sample A has been done for you. Do Sample B by yourself. When you are sure you know what to do, you may go on with the rest of the page.

Sample A:
- Ⓐ miccroscope
- Ⓑ mycroscope
- Ⓒ microscope
- Ⓓ mykroscope

Sample B:
- Ⓔ eequal
- Ⓕ equal
- Ⓖ equel
- Ⓗ equall

1. Ⓐ susppect Ⓑ sussppect Ⓒ susspect Ⓓ suspect

2. Ⓔ distract Ⓕ disstract Ⓖ disttract Ⓗ dissttract

3. Ⓐ export Ⓑ exxport Ⓒ exppport Ⓓ exporrt

4. Ⓔ insspect Ⓕ innspect Ⓖ inspect Ⓗ innsspect

5. Ⓐ spectater Ⓑ spectator Ⓒ specktator Ⓓ specktater

6. Ⓔ specktacle Ⓕ spectacle Ⓖ specttacle Ⓗ spectackle

7. Ⓐ subbttraction Ⓑ subttraction Ⓒ subbtraction Ⓓ subtraction

8. Ⓔ tractor Ⓕ tracter Ⓖ tracktor Ⓗ trackter

9. Ⓐ impport Ⓑ immport Ⓒ import Ⓓ importt

10. Ⓔ transsport Ⓕ transport Ⓖ transpport Ⓗ transsportt

11. Ⓐ transportashion Ⓑ transsportation Ⓒ transportation Ⓓ transporttation

12. Ⓔ attraction Ⓕ atraction Ⓖ attracktion Ⓗ attracshion

13. Ⓐ innspecter Ⓑ inspecter Ⓒ innspector Ⓓ inspector

14. Ⓔ missille Ⓕ misile Ⓖ missile Ⓗ misille

15. Ⓐ mishion Ⓑ mision Ⓒ mission Ⓓ misshion

16. Ⓔ committee Ⓕ comittee Ⓖ commitee Ⓗ comitee

17. Ⓐ intermishion Ⓑ intermisshion Ⓒ intermision Ⓓ intermission

18. Ⓔ porteble Ⓕ portable Ⓖ portabel Ⓗ portebel

19. Ⓐ respeckt Ⓑ resspect Ⓒ respect Ⓓ rispect

20. Ⓔ dismiss Ⓕ dissmiss Ⓖ dissmis Ⓗ dismis

Name ______________________

Fold back the paper along the dotted line. Use the blanks to write each word as it is read aloud. When you finish the test, unfold the paper. Use the list at the right to correct any spelling mistakes.

1. ______________ 1. clothes
2. ______________ 2. January
3. ______________ 3. cereal
4. ______________ 4. mortal
5. ______________ 5. lunar
6. ______________ 6. atlas
7. ______________ 7. ocean
8. ______________ 8. salute
9. ______________ 9. fury
10. ______________ 10. echo
11. ______________ 11. cycle
12. ______________ 12. cyclone
13. ______________ 13. gigantic
14. ______________ 14. Olympics
15. ______________ 15. territory
16. ______________ 16. terrace
17. ______________ 17. parasol
18. ______________ 18. fortune
19. ______________ 19. furious
20. ______________ 20. gracious

Review Words

21. ______________ 21. suspect
22. ______________ 22. inspect
23. ______________ 23. mission

Challenge Words

24. ______________ 24. jovial
25. ______________ 25. venerable

Name ________________________________

Using the Word Study Steps

1. LOOK at the word.
2. SAY the word aloud.
3. STUDY the letters in the word.
4. WRITE the word.
5. CHECK the word.
Did you spell the word right?
If not, go back to step 1.

territory	cycle	salute	furious
atlas	lunar	gigantic	echo
gracious	Olympics	fortune	ocean
terrace	parasol	mortal	cyclone
clothes	cereal	January	fury

A. Fill-Ins

Fill in the missing letters of each word to form a spelling word.

1. c ___ re ___ l
2. te ___ ra ___ e
3. gr ___ ___ ious
4. e ___ ___ o
5. gi ___ an ___ ic
6. o ___ e ___ n
7. at ___ ___ s
8. cl ___ t ___ es
9. ter ___ i ___ ory
10. p ___ ra ___ ol
11. mo ___ ___ al
12. f ___ ___ y
13. f ___ ___ ious
14. J ___ n ___ ___ ry
15. O ___ ___ mp ___ cs
16. s ___ lu ___ e
17. c ___ ___ le
18. cy ___ lo ___ e
19. l ___ n ___ r
20. for ___ ___ ___ e

B. Use the spelling words above to help you write a poem of at least four lines.

____

____

____

____

territory	cycle	salute	furious
atlas	lunar	gigantic	echo
gracious	Olympics	fortune	ocean
terrace	parasol	mortal	cyclone
clothes	cereal	January	fury

Sort each spelling word according to the number of syllables it contains. Then write the words on the lines below.

One syllable

1. ______________

Two syllables

2. ______________
3. ______________
4. ______________
5. ______________
6. ______________
7. ______________
8. ______________
9. ______________
10. ______________
11. ______________
12. ______________
13. ______________

Three syllables

14. ______________
15. ______________
16. ______________
17. ______________
18. ______________

Four syllables

19. ______________
20. ______________

Name ______________________________

territory	cycle	salute	furious
atlas	lunar	gigantic	echo
gracious	Olympics	fortune	ocean
terrace	parasol	mortal	cyclone
clothes	cereal	January	fury

A. Complete each sentence below with a spelling word. Use the word box to check your spelling.

1. Hannah helped raise money to build a ______________ playground.
2. Whether you win or lose, it's important to be ______________.
3. One famous athlete has his picture on a box of ______________.
4. The ______________ are held every four years in a different country.
5. You can look in an ______________ to find a map.
6. The new playground will not cost a ______________ to build.
7. You can hear the ______________ of your own voice if the Olympic stadium is empty.
8. Many athletes train by swimming in the ______________ during the warmer months.
9. Putting on ______________ can sometimes be challenging for people with disabilities.
10. The new school gym program will begin in ______________.

B. Write On!

Use each spelling word in a sentence.

11. parasol ______________________________
12. cyclone ______________________________
13. terrace ______________________________
14. mortal ______________________________
15. territory ______________________________

Name ______________________________

A. Circle the misspelled words in the passage. Write the words correctly on the lines below.

Jake heard his footsteps ecko as he walked into the jigantic stadium. Today he would compete in his first Olimpics. He had been training since Janyuary. He swam in the osean three times a week and had been watching his diet closely. This morning he had eaten a bowl of sereal and a piece of toast. The day he had been waiting for had finally come.

1. ________________ 3. ________________ 5. ________________

2. ________________ 4. ________________ 6. ________________

B. Writing Activity

Write a paragraph about a time when you helped someone accomplish a goal. Use four words from your spelling list.

____

____

____

____

____

____

____

____

____

____

____

____

____

____

Name ______________________________________

Look at the words in each set below. One word in each set is spelled correctly. Use a pencil to fill in the circle next to the correct word. Before you begin, look at the sample set of words. Sample A has been done for you. Do Sample B by yourself. When you are sure you know what to do, you may go on with the rest of the page.

Sample A:

Ⓐ Wednesday
Ⓑ Wendsday
Ⓒ Whendsday
Ⓓ Wensday

Sample B:

Ⓔ Satturday
Ⓕ Saturday
Ⓖ Satterday
Ⓗ Saterday

1. Ⓐ cerreal
Ⓑ sereal
Ⓒ cereal
Ⓓ cerial

2. Ⓔ terrase
Ⓕ terace
Ⓖ terrace
Ⓗ terase

3. Ⓐ gracious
Ⓑ grashious
Ⓒ graceious
Ⓓ grayshus

4. Ⓔ echoe
Ⓕ ecko
Ⓖ ecco
Ⓗ echo

5. Ⓐ giggantic
Ⓑ gigantic
Ⓒ jigantic
Ⓓ jiggantic

6. Ⓔ ocean
Ⓕ ohcean
Ⓖ oshun
Ⓗ oacean

7. Ⓐ attlas
Ⓑ atlass
Ⓒ atlas
Ⓓ attlass

8. Ⓔ cloathez
Ⓕ clothez
Ⓖ cloathes
Ⓗ clothes

9. Ⓐ territorry
Ⓑ territory
Ⓒ teritory
Ⓓ teritorry

10. Ⓔ parasol
Ⓕ parassol
Ⓖ parrasol
Ⓗ parasoll

11. Ⓐ moretal
Ⓑ mortle
Ⓒ mortel
Ⓓ mortal

12. Ⓔ fuery
Ⓕ fury
Ⓖ fuiry
Ⓗ furey

13. Ⓐ fuirious
Ⓑ fureious
Ⓒ furious
Ⓓ fuerious

14. Ⓔ January
Ⓕ Jannuary
Ⓖ Januery
Ⓗ Januarry

15. Ⓐ Olympicks
Ⓑ Olimpics
Ⓒ Ollympics
Ⓓ Olympics

16. Ⓔ selute
Ⓕ salute
Ⓖ sallute
Ⓗ sellute

17. Ⓐ cicle
Ⓑ scycle
Ⓒ cycle
Ⓓ scicle

18. Ⓔ cyclone
Ⓕ ciclone
Ⓖ scyclone
Ⓗ sciclone

19. Ⓐ loonar
Ⓑ luner
Ⓒ lunear
Ⓓ lunar

20. Ⓔ foretune
Ⓕ fortune
Ⓖ fourtune
Ⓗ fortun

Name ______________________________

Fold back the paper along the dotted line. Use the blanks to write each word as it is read aloud. When you finish the test, unfold the paper. Use the list at the right to correct any spelling mistakes.

	1. ________	1. tripod
	2. ________	2. triplet
	3. ________	3. unicorn
	4. ________	4. uniform
	5. ________	5. unison
	6. ________	6. biweekly
	7. ________	7. triple
	8. ________	8. bicycle
	9. ________	9. tricycle
	10. ________	10. unicycle
	11. ________	11. triangle
	12. ________	12. bisect
	13. ________	13. trio
	14. ________	14. unify
	15. ________	15. centipede
	16. ________	16. centimeter
	17. ________	17. century
	18. ________	18. binoculars
	19. ________	19. universe
	20. ________	20. university
Review Words	21. ________	21. cereal
	22. ________	22. terrace
	23. ________	23. atlas
Challenge Words	24. ________	24. bilingual
	25. ________	25. trilogy

Name ______________________________

Using the Word Study Steps

1. LOOK at the word.
2. SAY the word aloud.
3. STUDY the letters in the word.
4. WRITE the word.
5. CHECK the word.
   Did you spell the word right?
   If not, go back to step 1.

uniform	unison	bisect	tricycle
trio	tripod	university	unify
universe	biweekly	triangle	bicycle
binoculars	unicycle	centipede	unicorn
triplet	centimeter	triple	century

A. Find and Circle

Find and circle each of the spelling words in this puzzle. Words may read forward, backward, upward, downward, or diagonally.

E	N	B	B	E	S	N	N	K	N	C	J	K	O	T	J	T
U	D	P	I	I	R	R	A	R	I	O	T	G	R	I	R	E
N	E	E	U	S	W	Q	A	R	O	E	S	I	S	I	T	S
I	L	L	P	N	E	E	T	L	X	C	P	I	C	Y	R	R
F	P	L	O	I	I	C	E	F	U	L	I	Y	N	G	I	E
O	I	I	Z	Y	T	V	T	K	E	C	C	N	E	U	A	V
R	R	F	M	K	I	N	E	T	L	L	O	N	U	T	N	I
M	T	Y	F	I	N	U	E	R	E	Y	N	N	R	Q	G	N
E	L	C	Y	C	I	N	U	C	S	U	T	I	I	B	L	U
R	E	T	E	M	I	T	N	E	C	I	P	R	L	B	E	G
E	L	C	Y	C	I	B	A	L	K	O	T	I	I	C	M	R
C	E	N	T	U	R	Y	Q	B	D	D	D	Y	B	O	O	Q

Name ______________________________

uniform	unison	bisect	tricycle
trio	tripod	university	unify
universe	biweekly	triangle	bicycle
binoculars	unicycle	centipede	unicorn
triplet	centimeter	triple	century

Sort each spelling word according to its prefix. Then write the words on the lines below.

uni-

1. ____________
2. ____________
3. ____________
4. ____________
5. ____________
6. ____________
7. ____________

bi-

8. ____________
9. ____________
10. ____________
11. ____________

tri-

12. ____________
13. ____________
14. ____________
15. ____________
16. ____________
17. ____________

cent-

18. ____________
19. ____________
20. ____________

Name ______________________________

uniform	unison	bisect	tricycle
trio	tripod	university	unify
universe	biweekly	triangle	bicycle
binoculars	unicycle	centipede	unicorn
triplet	centimeter	triple	century

A. Definitions

Write the spelling word that has the same, or almost the same, meaning.

1. a name for three musical performers ________________
2. a wormlike animal with many pairs of legs ________________
3. an imaginary horselike animal with a single, long horn ________________
4. a figure with three sides and three angles ________________
5. occurring every two weeks ________________
6. a group or set of three ________________
7. a mode of transportation that has one wheel ________________
8. to cut into two equal parts ________________
9. a unit of length ________________
10. together or at the same time ________________

B. Fill in the Blanks

Complete each sentence with a spelling word. Use the word box to check your spelling.

11. Each member of the hotel staff wore a red ________________.
12. It would be strange to see a grownup riding a ________________.
13. Sports can bring people closer together and ________________ an entire state.
14. The old town hall was built over a ________________ ago.
15. The movie showed astronauts exploring the ________________.
16. Using ________________, you can see people far away.

A. Circle the misspelled words in the passage. Write the words correctly on the lines below.

The news show claimed it would be the cosmic event of the sentury, and I didn't want to miss it. After dark, I grabbed my bienoculars and headed out the door. I took a short bycycle ride to the park to get away from the street lights. Some students from the unaversity were already there. They had a telescope on a trypod, and I accepted their invitation to look into the sky with it. There, deep in the uneverse, a star was exploding. It didn't look like much from so far away, but I was glad to see it anyway.

1. ______________ 3. ______________ 5. ______________

2. ______________ 4. ______________ 6. ______________

B. Writing Activity

Write a paragraph about where you would go if you had a chance to travel anywhere in the universe. Use four words from your spelling list.

Name ______________________________

Look at the words in each set below. One word in each set is spelled correctly. Use a pencil to fill in the circle next to the correct word. Before you begin, look at the sample set of words. Sample A has been done for you. Do Sample B by yourself. When you are sure you know what to do, you may go on with the rest of the page.

Sample A:

Ⓐ byplane
Ⓑ biplane
Ⓒ bipplane
Ⓓ biplain

Sample B:

Ⓔ trident
Ⓕ triedent
Ⓖ trident
Ⓗ trydent

1. Ⓐ unnifform Ⓑ unniform Ⓒ unifform Ⓓ uniform
2. Ⓔ biesect Ⓕ bissect Ⓖ bisect Ⓗ bysect
3. Ⓐ trycycle Ⓑ triscyckle Ⓒ tricycle Ⓓ tricicle
4. Ⓔ triplet Ⓕ tripplet Ⓖ tripllet Ⓗ tripplIett
5. Ⓐ tripel Ⓑ tripple Ⓒ triple Ⓓ trippel
6. Ⓔ uniccorn Ⓕ unicorn Ⓖ unnicorn Ⓗ unicorrn
7. Ⓐ unify Ⓑ unnify Ⓒ unefy Ⓓ uniffy
8. Ⓔ unisson Ⓕ unnison Ⓖ unison Ⓗ unnisson
9. Ⓐ univearse Ⓑ unniverse Ⓒ univverse Ⓓ universe
10. Ⓔ unicycle Ⓕ unicicle Ⓖ uniscycle Ⓗ unnicycle
11. Ⓐ biweekly Ⓑ byweekly Ⓒ bieweekly Ⓓ biweakly
12. Ⓔ bynoculars Ⓕ binnoculars Ⓖ binoculars Ⓗ binocculars
13. Ⓐ tryangle Ⓑ triangel Ⓒ triangle Ⓓ trieangle
14. Ⓔ bisickle Ⓕ biecycle Ⓖ bycycle Ⓗ bicycle
15. Ⓐ trio Ⓑ treeo Ⓒ trieo Ⓓ tryo
16. Ⓔ centurry Ⓕ centtury Ⓖ century Ⓗ centturry
17. Ⓐ centipede Ⓑ centtipede Ⓒ centipeed Ⓓ centippede
18. Ⓔ centimetter Ⓕ centimmeter Ⓖ centimeter Ⓗ centimmetter
19. Ⓐ tripod Ⓑ triepod Ⓒ trypod Ⓓ trippod
20. Ⓔ universsity Ⓕ universeity Ⓖ univversity Ⓗ university

Name ______________________________

Fold back the paper along the dotted line. Use the blanks to write each word as it is read aloud. When you finish the test, unfold the paper. Use the list at the right to correct any spelling mistakes.

1.	______	1. enjoyable
2.	______	2. breakable
3.	______	3. favorable
4.	______	4. likable
5.	______	5. usable
6.	______	6. respectable
7.	______	7. affordable
8.	______	8. possible
9.	______	9. unreasonable
10.	______	10. laughable
11.	______	11. comfortable
12.	______	12. convertible
13.	______	13. invisible
14.	______	14. honorable
15.	______	15. capable
16.	______	16. sensible
17.	______	17. unbelievable
18.	______	18. bearable
19.	______	19. collapsible
20.	______	20. suitable
Review Words 21.	______	21. uniform
22.	______	22. bicycle
23.	______	23. triangle
Challenge Words 24.	______	24. manageable
25.	______	25. tangible

Name ____________________

Using the Word Study Steps

1. LOOK at the word.
2. SAY the word aloud.
3. STUDY the letters in the word.
4. WRITE the word.
5. CHECK the word.
   Did you spell the word right?
   If not, go back to step 1.

honorable	favorable	invisible	likable
enjoyable	collapsible	laughable	suitable
breakable	unbelievable	sensible	possible
convertible	affordable	respectable	comfortable
usable	bearable	unreasonable	capable

A. Fill-Ins

Fill in the missing letters of each word to form a spelling word.

1. collaps ___ ___ ___ e
2. break ___ ___ ___ e
3. afford ___ ___ ___ e
4. us ___ ___ ___ e
5. bear ___ ___ ___ e
6. favor ___ ___ ___ e
7. cap ___ ___ l ___
8. enjoy ___ ___ ___ ___
9. honor ___ ___ ___ e
10. convert ___ ___ ___ e
11. invis ___ ___ l ___
12. unreason ___ ___ l ___
13. respect ___ ___ ___ e
14. sens ___ ___ l ___
15. unbeliev ___ ___ ___ e
16. poss ___ ___ l ___
17. suit ___ ___ ___ e
18. laugh ___ ___ ___ ___
19. lik ___ ___ ___ ___
20. comfort ___ ___ ___ ___

B. Alphabetical Order

Use the lines below to write the spelling words in alphabetical order.

1. ________	6. ________	11. ________	16. ________
2. ________	7. ________	12. ________	17. ________
3. ________	8. ________	13. ________	18. ________
4. ________	9. ________	14. ________	19. ________
5. ________	10. ________	15. ________	20. ________

Name ______________________________

honorable	favorable	invisible	likable
enjoyable	collapsible	laughable	suitable
breakable	unbelievable	sensible	possible
convertible	affordable	respectable	comfortable
usable	bearable	unreasonable	capable

A. Sort each spelling word according to its ending. Then write the words on the lines below.

-able

1. ______________ 6. ______________ 11. ______________
2. ______________ 7. ______________ 12. ______________
3. ______________ 8. ______________ 13. ______________
4. ______________ 9. ______________ 14. ______________
5. ______________ 10. ______________ 15. ______________

-ible

16. ______________ 19. ______________
17. ______________ 20. ______________
18. ______________

B. Make a Puzzle

Make up a puzzle of your own using the space on this page. Give it to someone else to solve. Be sure to include at least five spelling words in your puzzle.

Name ________________________________

honorable	usable	affordable	sensible	suitable
enjoyable	favorable	bearable	respectable	possible
breakable	collapsible	invisible	unreasonable	comfortable
convertible	unbelievable	laughable	likable	capable

A. Sentence Completions

Complete each sentence below with a spelling word. Use the word box to check your spelling.

1. Many tiny creatures are ______________ to the human eye.
2. Marcus likes surfing and finds any day at the beach to be ______________.
3. The campers had a ______________ tent that could fold up quickly.
4. Those delicate glass sculptures are __________, so be careful with them.
5. Maneesha is a ______________ athlete who can play many sports.
6. That broken stove is not ______________ and needs to be fixed.
7. She is a ______________ reporter because her work is always well researched.
8. Being a doctor is an ______________ job because it helps people stay healthy.
9. Some colleges are expensive, but others are more ______________.
10. We had never seen so much snow before—it was ___________!

B. Similar Meanings

Write the spelling word that has the same, or almost the same, meaning.

11. cozy ______________
12. pleasant ______________
13. capable of being dealt with ______________
14. not practical ______________
15. having good sense ______________
16. capable of happening ______________
17. funny ______________
18. proper ______________

A. Circle the misspelled words in the passage. Write the words correctly on the lines provided.

Welcome to the Hawaii Science College! We do our best to make getting a science degree affordible for everyone. You will find the cost of our classes is not unreasonble. Also, we want your time here as a student to be enjoyabl. Our teachers are likeble people who will help you meet the challenge of college-level homework. With a degree from our school, anything is possable! So let's start the tour. Please let me know whether we can do anything to make your visit here more comfortible.

1. ______________ 3. ______________ 5. ______________

2. ______________ 4. ______________ 6. ______________

B. Writing Activity

Write a paragraph about your favorite outdoor activity or school subject. Use four words from your spelling list.

____

____

____

____

____

____

____

____

____

____

____

____

____

Name ___________________________________

Look at the words in each set below. One word in each set is spelled correctly. Use a pencil to fill in the circle next to the correct word. Before you begin, look at the sample set of words. Sample A has been done for you. Do Sample B by yourself. When you are sure you know what to do, you may go on with the rest of the page.

Sample A:
Ⓐ invinceable
Ⓑ invincable
Ⓒ invincible
Ⓓ invinceible

Sample B:
Ⓔ dooible
Ⓕ doible
Ⓖ doable
Ⓗ dooable

1. Ⓐ collapseable Ⓑ collapseible Ⓒ collapsible Ⓓ collapsable
2. Ⓔ breakable Ⓕ breakible Ⓖ brakeable Ⓗ brakeible
3. Ⓐ affordable Ⓑ afordable Ⓒ affordible Ⓓ afordible
4. Ⓔ usabel Ⓕ useible Ⓖ usible Ⓗ usable
5. Ⓐ bearible Ⓑ bearable Ⓒ bearrable Ⓓ bearrible
6. Ⓔ favoreable Ⓕ favorible Ⓖ favorable Ⓗ favoreible
7. Ⓐ capeible Ⓑ capeable Ⓒ capable Ⓓ capible
8. Ⓔ enjoyyible Ⓕ enjoyyable Ⓖ enjoyible Ⓗ enjoyable
9. Ⓐ honorible Ⓑ honorable Ⓒ honorrable Ⓓ honorrible
10. Ⓔ convertible Ⓕ convertable Ⓖ converttible Ⓗ converttable
11. Ⓐ invisible Ⓑ invisable Ⓒ invissible Ⓓ inivissable
12. Ⓔ unreasonnable Ⓕ unreasonible Ⓖ unreasonable Ⓗ unreasonnible
13. Ⓐ respectible Ⓑ respectable Ⓒ respecttible Ⓓ respecttable
14. Ⓔ senseable Ⓕ sensable Ⓖ senseible Ⓗ sensible
15. Ⓐ unbelievible Ⓑ unbelieveible Ⓒ unbelieveable Ⓓ unbelievable
16. Ⓔ possible Ⓕ possable Ⓖ posible Ⓗ posable
17. Ⓐ suitible Ⓑ suitable Ⓒ suiteable Ⓓ suiteible
18. Ⓔ laghable Ⓕ laghible Ⓖ laughible Ⓗ laughable
19. Ⓐ likeible Ⓑ likable Ⓒ likible Ⓓ likkable
20. Ⓔ comforttable Ⓕ comforttible Ⓖ comfortible Ⓗ comfortable